Heinkel He 111H

The development of the He 111 hearkens back to a small, yet racy-looking sport plane, the Baümer "Sausewind", and the He 64 two-seat light aircraft. Their design principles matured into the well-known He 70 "Blitz", a high-speed passenger and reconnaissance airplane. The development of these and many other designs are inexorably tied to such names as Prof. Ernst Heinkel, the brothers Walter and Siegfried Günther and Karl Schwärzler.

On 24 February 1935 the first prototype, designated then as the He 111 A (= He 111 V1), carried out its first successful test flight at the hands of Heinkel's chief test pilot, Gerhard Nitschke.

The first production models were manufactured as the He 111 A-1 in 1936 and could carry a 1000 kg bomb load over a distance of 1,100 km at an average speed of 330 kmh. This gave a maximum penetration range of approximately 500 km. These performance figures, however, did not meet up to the expectations of the Luftwaffe or the RLM and the aircraft was therefore approved for export to China.

The He 111 B followed a year later; instead of the BMW VI inline engines it was equipped with two DB 600 Cs and could carry 2000 kg of bombs to its target, although only to a distance of 650 km. Thanks to the new inline engines, however, the cruising speed increased by 45 kmh from 330 kmh to 375 kmh.

The He 111 B spawned the J-series in 1936 and the F-series in 1937. These new versions were fitted with the DB 600 G and the Jumo 211A and had a new outer wing of stressed-skin construction.

Barely a year later there followed the large-scale production of the He 111 P series, powered by two DB 601 A engines. This version's distinguishing characteristics included a spacious all-round view canopy, retractable radiators and a completely hydraulic retractable landing gear. As a result of its increased airborne weight (12,700 kg) the aircraft was a bit slower than the He 111 F. Between 1939 and 1944 twenty-three versions of the He 111 H were added to previous versions, and plans were made to eventually develop the He 111 R-1 and R-2 — aircraft which would have attained a speed of 490 kmh with a 1000 kg external bomb load. However, as the fortunes of war changed, by the summer of 1944 all production of the improved-performance He 111 series had been halted in favor of high-performance aircraft (Ar 234 and Me 262). And so concludes the condensed version of the He 111's developmental history.

The first models of the He 111 H, completed just before the beginning of the war, at first made their way quite reluctantly to the Luftwaffe's bomber units. The majority of aircraft were required for numerous evaluation tests at the test facility in Rechlin on the Müritz. A modified He 111 P-1 served as the initial prototype for the He 111 H-1 and was still equipped with that version's two DB 601 A inline engines (later changed to the Jumo 211 A-1 powerplants).

The first He 111 with an all-view canopy most likely stemmed from the He 111 V7, which successfully completed its maiden flight in early 1939. Unlike the He 111 P models with their DB 601s, the H-series were fitted from the outset with two Jumo 211 A-1 inline engines. Otherwise the fuselage was nearly identical to that of the He 111 P-2.

The breakdown and displacement of German bomber units equipped with the He 111 H (and P) was as follows in August 1939:

- I./KG 1 "Hindenburg", Kolberg
- I./KG 4 "General Wever", Gotha
- II./KG 4 "General Wever", Erfurt
- III./KG 4 "General Wever", Nordhausen
- I./KG 26 "Löwengeschwader", Lübeck
- II./KG 26 "Löwengeschwader", Lüneburg
- I./KG 27 "Boelcke", Hannover
- II./KG 27 "Boelcke", Wunstorf
- II./KG 27 "Boelcke", Delmenhorst

An He 111 F-4 in the spring of 1938. This version had the same ordnance system as the E-4 series.

- II./KG 28, Gütersloh
- I./KG 51 "Edelweiss", Landsberg
- III./KG 51 "Edelweiss" Memmingen
- I./KG 53 "Legion Condor", Ansbach
- II./KG 53 "Legion Condor", Schwäbisch Hall
- III./KG 53 "Legion Condor", Giebelstadt
- I./KG 54 "Totenkopfgeschwader", Fritzlar
- I./KG55 "Greifengeschwader", Langendiebach
- II./KG 55 "Greifengeschwader", Giessen
- II./Kg 77, Olmütz
- II.(K)/LG 1 "Lehrgeschwader", Schwerin
- III.(K)/LG 1 "Lehrgeschwader", Greifswald
- 2./InAbtlg. 100 (KGr. 100), Köthen

On 2 September 1939 there were 787 He 111s available to the Luftwaffe's bomber units. This amounted to a total of 67% of the entire bomber inventory! This included 38 E-series aircraft, 346 P-series and 400 He 111 H-1 and H-2 models; roughly half the units therefore flew He 111 Ps, the other half either the He 111 H-1 or the H-2.

The **He 111 H-1** was the first model of the new H-series. However, barely 100 of this type were produced by Heinkel. The armament consisted solely of three MG 15s, which equipped the nose, dorsal and ventral gun positions. This defensive armament was found to be inadequate even as early as the Polish campaign. This resulted in some of the aircraft being fitted with a machine gun in each of the two side windows. The aircraft was capable of carrying a bomb load of up to 2000 kg in the internal bomb bay. External racks, or ETCs, were not available for versions prior to the He 111 H-4.

Several of the He 111 H-1 series were operated as training aircraft for maritime operations and were designated H-2/R-1 after being fitted with an improved radio set. A portion of these aircraft were later converted back to the standard bomber configuration. At the end of operations against Poland the He 111 H-1 aircraft were turned over to auxiliary and training squadrons to complete their service life there. Examples of some of these units (according to loss records) are the KG 100 auxiliary combat training flight, the KG 26 auxiliary combat training squadron and the training squadron for KG 53.

Shortly before the war's outbreak the powerplant of the He 111 H-1 was changed from the Jumo 211 A-1 to the higher-performing A-3 variant. This was the basic differentiating characteristic of the H-2 from its predecessor. Better flight performance was achieved thanks to the new engine and the increased defensive armament gave the H-2 better protection than the H-1.

A number of the aircraft delivered were the modified He 111 H-1/R-3 series. Defensive weaponry — as mentioned earlier — was increased by two MG 15 in side window mounts beginning in 1939, based on experience from the Polish campaign. In the event that an additional machine gun was to be installed in the ventral gondola pointing in the direction of flight the aircraft was designated H-2/R-2. A few were also later fitted with an extendible radio-jamming rod in the tail and were designated as the He 111 H-2/R-3.

Altogether approximately 500 H-1 and H-2 versions were built. The H-3 and H-10 were later modifications of these aircraft. The H-2 was also used in the role of long-range reconnaissance. A few of the machines were therefore fitted with automatic aerial photography equipment in Oranienburg and transferred to the "Gruppe Rowehl", which later became the reconnaissance group for the ObdL. (Commander-in-chief of the Luftwaffe). The first batch of He 111 H-2s assigned for reconnaissance duties was initially operated by the third squadron of Gruppe Rowehl. The camera equipment was installed in the front portion of the gondola, as revealed by air-to-air photos of an H-2. In addition to the ObdL's reconnaissance group He 111 H versions were occasionally operated by Aufklärungsgruppen 121 and 123. Heinkel reconnaissance planes were also utilized in great numbers with 2., 4. and 5.(F)/Fernaufklärungsgruppe 122 during the first years of the war. In the summer of 1944 He 111 H reconnaissance aircraft were still known to be operating with 4.(F)/11 where they, along with a few Ju 88s, flew from Baranovichi on wide-ranging reconnaissance missions over the Eastern Front. Together with the Do 217 the He 111 was flown by a night reconnaissance unit, Nachtaufklärungsstaffel 1 from Foscani, Italy. In addition, the He 111 H operated with Wettererkundungsstaffeln 5, 6, 26, 51 and 76, flying armed weather reconnaissance missions over all fronts.

The He 111 H-3 supplemented the earlier, relatively common versions beginning in November of 1939. All changes introduced up to and including the H-14 were simply variations of the H-3 version. Series production of this type mainly took place at the Oranienburg factory. With the exception of the powerplants the aircraft were virtually identical to the

The He 111 A did not meet the performance requirements of the RLM.

He 111 H-1 and H-2. In place of the two Jumo 211 A-3s the H-3 was given two Jumo 211 D-1 engines. The most important advantage of this change was the improvement in longer single-engine flight potential. Armament was the same as for the H-2. A few H-3s were fitted with extra armor and flew — with an MG FF in the nose gun position ("A-Stand") — sporadic strafing missions. Some of these aircraft simply had the MG 15 in place of the 20 mm cannon. Production designation then became the He 111 H-3/R-2. If the airplane were fitted with an MG 131 in the nose position it was listed under the designation of H-3/R-4. Gondola armament initially consisted solely of an MG 15 pointed to the rear. Due to later modification directives this was beefed up to include installation of an additional MG 15 or an MG 131 (He 111 H-3/R-3). Standard bomb load was usually up to eight SC 250 general purpose bombs. Following missions flown during Operation "Weserübung" (Denmark and Norway), during which numerous sorties were flown against ship targets, it was learned that the passive armor for the crew was inadequate.

More than 350 He 111 H-3 aircraft were produced between 1939 and 1940. Starting at the end of September 1940 Heinkel's **He 111 H-4** began replacing the earlier H-3, if only in limited numbers. This machine was a near copy of its predecessor, but had the capability of swapping the internal 2 x 4 ESAC vertical bomb racks for two PVC 1006 racks outboard of the fuselage, used to carry heavy external loads such as the SC 1000 or SC 1800 bombs. The potential fuselage load was thereby restricted to four 250 kg bombs, although the bomb bay was often empty due to weight limit restrictions. Alternatively, instead of carrying two of the heaviest bomb calibers it was possible to carry the four SC 250s in the bomb bay and an SC 1000 below the fuselage.

Barely 150 He 111 H-4s left the assembly lines. The limited-production H-4 was followed in February 1941 by the **He 111 H-5**. This variant of the twin-engine bomber was powered either by the Jumo 211 D or, later, the Jumo 211 H inline engine. The H-5 was in all other respects similar to the preceding version, particularly when it came to ordnance load. The majority of the aircraft supplied only spent a relatively short period of time with the bomber units due to the arrival of the better-performing H-6.

For the night-bomber role the He 111 H-5 could either carry a heavy bomb load with the two PVC 1006s or a single bomb of heavy caliber and six 50 kg parachute flares. As a result of the two heavy bombs and the weight of the passive armor the performance figures for the H-5 were considerably less than those for a fully loaded He 111 H-3. In addition to a bomber role the H-5 also could operate as a day time or nighttime long-range reconnaissance aircraft. For these operations the plane was fitted with either a Type Rb 30/30 or Rb 50/30 aerial photography camera. It was also possible for the aircraft to carry up to six 50 kg LC 50 F parachute-retarded flares. The ability to carry the heaviest types of bombs caused the all-up weight for the He 111 H-5 to climb to over 14,000 kg. For the pilot, this surely meant the maxi-

Flying operations at an advanced flight training school.

The He 111 V8 (D-AQUO) had neither a ventral gun position (gondola) nor a partially enclosed dorsal gun position.

mum weight possible for takeoff. Between 1940 and 1941 approximately 500 He 111 H-5 airplanes were produced and delivered to the bomber units. The first He 111 to be shot down, an H-4 with the WerkNr. (serial number) 3232, was destroyed on the morning of 3 February 1940 by the well-known Hurricane pilot Peter Townsend. The aircraft was on the charge of KG 26.

The Luftwaffe sacrificed roughly 200 He 111 H-2 through H-4s during the bitter air battles that took place in the skies over England between July and October 1940. It is known that the first He 111 lost during the Battle of Britain was an H-2 which fell on 10 July 1940. The crew of Lt. Kupfer from III./KG 53 was shot down in air combat by an RAF fighter.

The first He 111 H-3 to be lost over the English mainland was 1H + FT (9./KG 26) which failed to return from a combat mission on 12 July 1940.

The first He 111 H-4 was shot down by RAF fighters on 11 September 1940. In addition to four He 111 H-4s, including WerkNr. 6962 whose crew were taken captive, this was also the fate of three further H-4s from 1./KG 26. On the same day 2/KG 26 lost four He 111 H-3s, with 3./KG 26 sacrificing an additional two bombers. The Geschwader's II Gruppe was also used in the battle and lost five He 111 H-3s and H-5s during a mission.

Probably the first He 111 H-5 which failed to return from a combat mission over England was WerkNr. 3510, which collided with a barrage balloon and crashed.

Following behind the H-3, the **He 111 H-6** was the second large-scale production version of Heinkel's bomber and was based on the H-4. The prototype model for this development was the He 111 V25. As with the He 111 H-4, this version was also equipped with PVC racks for carrying heavy ordnance; these could be used for testing aerial torpedoes in combat units. The H-6 had the same armament as the H-5, but was fitted with the more powerful Jumo 211 F-1 in place of the Jumo 211 D-1 and had fully automatic variable pitch Junkers VS 11 propellers. These were controlled by an electro-hydraulic r.p.m. governor which maintained the revolutions between 1700 and 2600 r.p.m. by means of an adjusting lever. The F-1 engine possessed automatic turbocharger activation as well as an automatically working mixture controller. Later the Jumo 211 F-1 was replaced by the stronger F-2 version of the engine. The fuel system for all He 111 H-6s was taken directly from the H-5.

Radio communications systems for the He 111 H-6 were initially nearly the same as those of the H-5, but over a period of time was fitted with Patin automatic direction-finding equipment, the FuG 25a identification friend-or-foe system and, from late summer 1941 on, the FuG 16 and 28 as well as a precision altimeter.

Defensive armament consisted of two MG 15s in the nose, an additional machine gun in the dorsal gun position("B-Stand"), one in the gondola("C-Stand") and two to the left and right of the radio equipment. Some He 111 H-6s were fitted with an supplemental MG FF in the gondola as well. Occasionally, an MG 17 could also be found installed in the tail.

The ordnance delivery system enabled loads of up to 2,000 kg to be carried; alternatively, two LT-5b aerial torpedoes (each weighing 765 kg) or LMA and LMB aerial mines (weighing 500 and 1000 kg respectively) could also be dropped.

The airborne torpedo attack played an utterly insignificant role during the first years of the war, a fact that can be attributed to the long-standing conflict whereby Wehrmacht assets were eventually attached to naval aviation units and the considerable technical problems encountered with aerial torpedoes. Such was the case on 2 June 1941 when only one of the Luftwaffe's three He 111 torpedo bombers was operationally ready. This carried out an unsuccessful attack against a merchant vessel that had been mistaken for an aircraft carrier. It was only through intensive Italian and Japanese support that the Luftwaffe was eventually able to field better functioning, relatively reliable torpedoes (such as the LT F-5b, etc.), although these were by no means completely problem-free.

The main task for the KG 26 "Löwenherz" bomber unit with regard to aerial torpedo operations was to engage shipping targets in the Mediterranean, the North Sea and the Baltic. In January 1940 KG 26 formed 7./KG 26 from the 3./309 (Mehrzweck) for mine-laying operations. In February 1941 6./KG 26 at first received He 111 H-4 torpedo carriers, which were eventually replaced in part by the He 111 H-6. In January 1942 the Staffel was transferred to the Black Sea and flew torpedo missions there. The results of these attacks led to the entire I. Gruppe being equipped with H-6 torpedo bombers. In April of 1942 the long-overdue conversion of II./KG 26 also took place. At the same time III. Gruppe was given the Ju 88 A-4 as a torpedo bomber. By March 1944 the first two Gruppen had also converted to the better-performing Ju 88 A-4 and A-17, with the first Ju 188 being assigned to KG 26 in August 1944. Under the command of Oberstleutnant Georg Teske KG 26 continued to operate over water right up to the war's end from bases in Denmark and Norway. At least one He 111 H continued to be used by the unit for transport duties for a long time.

Performance was 410 kmh at 4000 m altitude; at an altitude of 5000 m a speed of 410 kmh could be

D-AYWQ, a prototype, was one of the first aircraft with a fully glazed nose.

attained. At 5000 m and with a cruising speed of 380 kmh, the bomber had a range of nearly 2000 km.

The He 111 H-6 saw service with nearly all the Luftwaffe's Kampfgeschwadern. This included KG 1 "Hindenburg", KG 4 "General Wever", KG 26 "Löwengeschwader", KG 53 "Legion Condor", KG 55 "Greifengeschwader" and the KG 100 "Wiking", which was the former Kampfgruppe 100. Except for maritime operations, the majority of these units were concentrated on the Eastern Front to support the advancing forces of the Wehrmacht. As the fortunes of war began to turn the units were chiefly used — where possible — for relief attacks and supply flights along the Eastern Front. An example of this was the use of KG 4 for simultaneous bombing and supply missions in the vicinity of the Kholm pocket. The Demyansk pocket was supplied from March 1942 not only by the three-engine Ju 52s from the various Kampfgruppen z.b.V. (special tasking combat groups), but also by the He 111-equipped Kampfgruppe z.b.V. 7 led by Hptm. Zahn. Air transport in the VIII Fliegergruppe's area of operations was provided by Major Uhl's Kampfgruppe z.b.V. 5, established in mid-November 1942. From this and other He 111 units the "Gruppe Uhl" was later formed, surviving until the end of the war.

It was initially the He 111s of Kampfgruppe z.b.V. 5, eventually joined by many other He 111 H Kampfgeschwader units on the Eastern Front, which carried out operations above the Red Army's pincer movement around Stalingrad which had begun on 20 November 1942. According to a report by Generalingenieur Weindinger from Luftflotte 4, on 24 January 1943 there were still 55 He 111 Hs available for supply operations. The status of an additional 104 Heinkel bombers was uncertain, most of these having wheel or tail-skid damage. Within three days, however, 35 of these were back in operation.

When radio communications were broken off with AOK 6 (the Stalingrad army) on 2 February 1943, twelve He 111s flew with supply packets for the last time over the devastated city. However, the crews couldn't find a target to drop their loads on due to the bad weather and the numerous fires in the city center.

From the war journal of HQ Milch it is known that in addition to 266 Ju 52s and 57 various other types, 165 He 111s were lost during the supply operations over Stalingrad (Volgograd) between 24 January 1942 and 31 January 1943. The Luftwaffe had lost a total of 488 aircraft — the equivalent of several Geschwader.

Of these losses, 166 airplanes alone had to be written off completely. An additional 108 were listed as missing over the vast white expanse of the Eastern Front's southern sector. A total of 214 aircraft, including many He 111s, crashed during takeoff or landing and were no longer repairable. The loss ratio was the lowest for the He 111, with 5.5% of those participating in operations; the Ju 52 rate was 10.0%, and the He 177 had the highest with 26.0%

Numerous He 111 H bombers were also used as tow aircraft for the Go 242 during supply operations for the Kholm (May 1942) and Velikiye Luki (December 1942/January 1943) pockets, as well as for 2 Armee's "wandering pocket" (early 1943). Additionally, He 111 Hs were represented in consider-

Close-up of the He 111 H-1 canopy with an MG 15 in the nose gunner's position. Bomb bay doors are clearly visible.

This He 111 H-1 belonged to KG 27.

Some He 111 H-1s were employed — after conversion — as pathfinders with Kampfgruppe 100 for bomber operations against England.

A rather unusual helmet at KGr. 100.

able numbers with airborne units, which also operated them as tow aircraft. 71 He 111s flew with XI. Fliegerkorps alone in various units and training schools. But on 10 August 1943 only 30 of these Heinkel bombers were listed as operationally ready:

- HQ. Fliegerführer IX. Fliegerkorps
- Transportstaffel IX. Fliegerkorps
- Fallschirmschule I
- Fallschirmschule II
- Fallschirmschule II (Operational)
- GS — Kommando 1
- GS — Kommando 2
- I./Luftlandegeschwader 2

In addition to the later H-16 the He 111 H-6 had the largest dissemination among the Luftwaffe's bomber units. Between 1941 and 1942 nearly 1,800 aircraft of this type were produced for many varied roles.

The follow-on **He 111 H-7** was simply a subtype of the H-6 which dispensed with the MG 17 in the tail. This applied to the tail's entire weapon system (including ammunition feed and gun mounts). This was basically, then, no more than a modification of the H-6. The next version was simply a conversion of existing types. The **He 111 H-8** was produced with balloon cable deflectors and existed in two models. The He 111 H-8 was derived from either the H-3 or H-5, of which a total of 30 aircraft were converted with the Jumo 211 D-1 inline engine. Thus configured, the type was designated H-8/R-1. As a result of the weighty protuberance a counterbalance was installed in the fuselage of the He 111 H-8. This caused the flight performance of the H-8 version to drop drastically. Later the cumbersome cutting equipment was done away with thanks to the introduction of the so-called "Kutonase" balloon cable cutters on the H-8, a device that was able to cut through steel cable up to 6 mm thick.

The next version of the He 111 was also a modification of existing aircraft variants. The **He 111 H-9**, a modified H-6 was fitted on the production line with a so-called Kutonase in place of the restrictive balloon deflector and corresponded to either the He 111 H-5 or the H-8, depending on which version the sub-type was based. In addition, the aircraft was fitted with the higher-performing Jumo 211 F-1 inline engine. Some of these aircraft were utilized for the quite costly low-level attacks in the Mediterranean area.

As with the H-9, the **He 111 H-10** was a direct follow-on modification development of the He 111 H-6. The first of these aircraft became operational in large numbers only after the spring of 1943, however. As far as equipment, both versions were nearly identical except for the lack of external bomb racks. Wings were fitted with the Kutonase balloon cutters as on the H-9 earlier.

In addition, the H-10 had an improved semi-armored dorsal gunner's position, which was now fully enclosed. The MG 15 had in its stead the more commonly found MG 131; less frequent was an MG 81 Z. The aircraft fitted with the MG 81 were designated He 111 H-10/R-2. The performance figures for the H-10 rose somewhat thanks to the fact that the external loads were dispensed with. The entire load of ordnance had to be carried internally within a four-section vertical bomb bay inside the fuselage. Two Jumo 211 F-1 or F-2 with turbochargers were installed in the aircraft.

The next new production version of the reliable level bomber following the He 111 H-6 was the **He 111 H-11**. Between the end of 1941 and the summer of 1943 at least 510 He 111 H-11s were built. The new bomber was based on the He 111 V32 and V33 prototypes. This bomber was also a derivative of the He 111 H-6. The majority of the early H-11s were taken from airplanes of the H-6 series and equipped with a multi-purpose bomb rack beneath the center fuselage for carrying up to five SC 250 bombs.

For a short period, large-size fuselage art such as this could be found at KG 27.

Empennage of an He 111 H-1 during the Polish campaign.

A pathfinder (using the "X" method) of KGr. 100 enroute to England.

Alternatively, the He 111 H-11/R-3 possessed five individual ETC racks which could be exchanged for two PVC heavy racks as needed. Since the inner vertical racks were removed out of necessity in both cases, fuel capacity could be increased significantly with the addition of one or two auxiliary tanks in their place. Defensive firepower on the H-11 was improved considerably with the first-time installation of an MG 81 Z in the gondola in place of the MG 15. There was no longer an MG 17 or radio jamming equipment fitted since this defensive weaponry wasn't always adequate for the needs of the troops. The He 111 H-11 was distinguished by a fully enclosed dorsal gunner's position sporting an MG 131 Illing machine gun pivoting on an armored WL-131 AL ball mount. Combat units sometimes replaced the side MG 15 guns with MG 81 Zs. In this case the aircraft were designated He 111 H-11/R-1. Some of these aircraft were used as tow planes and were fitted with towing gear. Aircraft with this equipment carried the designation He 111 H-11/R-2.

The following version was yet another specialized variant of the He 111 H-6. The **He 111 H-12** was the first He 111 H which did not have a gondola as a ventral gun position. The aircraft were originally designed for the use of glide bombs (Hs 293) and remotely guided ordnance (PC-1400 X). Since the inadequate range of this version ruled out successful offensive operations over water, only a relatively small number of aircraft were converted to H-12 standards and for the most part were operated over the Baltic Sea testing these new types of ordnance. The H-12, which was eventually flown mainly as a trainer, was converted from available He 111 H-6s by Weserflug GmbH in Bremen.

The He 111 H-12/R-1 version was a bomber designed to operate with a glide bomb, such as the Hs 293 A-1 or the Hs 294. Aircraft which were designed to carry the PC-1400 X guided bomb carried the designation He 111 H-12/R-2.

Operations with the new specialized weapons dictated an increase in radio gear. In addition to the normally installed radio equipment, this included the following components: FuG 203 A (Kehl I), FuG 203 B (Kehl II), or the FuG 203 C (Kehl III). The practical and in conjunction, the tactical testing of the PC-1400 X ("Fritz X") took place in Cazeaux starting on 18 August 1942. As a result of the disbandment of Erprobungskommando 15 and diverse technical problems, tests with the "Fritz X" were carried out only sporadically until the summer of 1943 — in great part due to the fact that new technical territory was constantly being breached.

Development of the various models of the Hs 293 also proceeded at a slow pace. Since He 111 H-12 operations with the Hs 293 were deemed unreliable from a tactical point of view, the aircraft were

A typical propaganda photo from 1940.

WerkNr. 5101, an He 111 H-1, is an example of one of KGr. 100's "three-masted" pathfinder aircraft.

He 111 bomber formation over southern England, August 1940.

Several tests using skis were carried out in 1941 using He 111 H-1 (6N + AX).

This He 111 H-1 of KGr. 100 was camouflaged in black for pathfinder duties at night.

An early He 111 H-3 in Norway. The aircraft already has a forward-firing gun in the gondola.

Compensating an He 111 H-2 converted from an H-1 of Stab KGr. 100. Western Front, 1940.

used exclusively for training the operating crews. Flight tactics training was initially carried out by personnel of the Lehr and Erprobungskommando 15 and took place in Peenemünde. Familiarization training was conducted with the He 111 H-12 in Anklam. In addition, flights were carried out from Jesau near Königsberg. The He 111 H-12's actual tactical missions were flown by the Do 217 E-5, K-2 and K-3 as well as the He 177 A-3 and A-5. An attempt to use the Fw 200 C as a guided weapons platform was deemed a failure during test flights.

The He 111 H-10 (a modification of the H-6) provided the basis for a further modification — along with the He 111 H-4 — of a small number of prototype aircraft for the new **He 111 H-14** series. These were supplemented by a production run of 50 purpose-built aircraft of this type.

The aircraft were equipped with an expanded suite of radio equipment for offensive operations over water. This included the FuG 16, FuMB 4 "Samos", a radio intercept receiver as well as a Peil GV radar homing device with an APZ 5. In addition, an FuG 351 "Korfu" was included which also served as an intercept receiver. Together with the similarly converted H-4s the H-14 airplanes were combined to form "Kommando Rastedter" in Bordeaux-Merignac and operated over the Bay of Biscay and the Atlantic. Following the losses suffered during these missions the remaining aircraft were pulled out of service and — after the radio equipment was removed — distributed among several bomber units on the Eastern Front.

Many aircraft were converted to the He 111 H-18 standard and thereafter carried the designation of H-18/R-3. Several of these were operated by KG 40. Enemy action resulted in the loss of many H-18s, and soon the remaining aircraft were pulled out of action due to the limited tactical application possibilities.

Approximately 20 to 30 of the He 111 H-14 manufactured were subsequently fitted with tow equipment for pulling transport gliders, entering service as the H-14/R-2. Further modification of available aircraft eventually resulted in the **He 111 H-15**, an aircraft which was to be used both as a pathfinder and, at the same time, have the ability to carry remotely guided weapons. It is not known whether the concept resulted in a prototype.

After the He 111 H-3, H-6 and H-11, the **He 111 H-16** was the fourth largest production version of Heinkel's twin-engine bomber design. The aircraft was a direct descendant of the H-11. Two Jumo 211 F-1s served as powerplants. Auxiliary fuel tanks could be fitted inside the bomb bay in order to provide a significant increase in the tactical range capability.

The He 111 H-16, which made up the greatest percentage of the current production aircraft from 1942 on, carried the same type of defensive armament as the H-6 — with the exception of the MG 131 B2. The He 111 H-16/R-1 was fitted with a DL 131 mounted on a scarf ring in the dorsal gunner's station, giving the gunner a 360-degree field of fire. The

This He 111 H-2 belonged to 7./KG 27 (IV. Fliegerkorps)

Combat aircraft of KG 55 during a mission over England.

weapon was equipped with a gun stop in the region of the vertical stabilizer in order to prevent damage to the aircraft. This sub-type was additionally fitted with an MG 131 on a WL/BR roller-type machine gun mount in place of the MG FF in the nose. There was no weapon installed in the gondola's forward ventral gun position. The rear ventral gun position was equipped with an MG 81 Z. The nose glazing was improved in critical areas and the armored glass was given a coating of quite effective anti-glare material. In cases were the airplane was fitted with increased armor protection at the expense of bomb load capacity, it was designated as He 111 H-16/R-3.

Since it was anticipated that various H-16 models would be used in the role of transport glider tow-

This He 111 H-2 (or H-3) barely managed to return home after a mission over England.

A wealth of bombs laid out in front of an He 111 H-3 of 7./KG 53. France, summer 1940.

In 1940 this He 111 H-2 was part of KG 53's inventory, stationed in northern France.

The Wetteraufklärungsstaffeln (Westa's, or weather reconnaissance squadrons) were equipped with the He 111 H-2 during the first years of the war; depicted here is 1B + FH of Westa 2.

ing, these were given additional defensive armor in the form of an MG 15 in the gondola. The tow aircraft were then designated He 111 H-16/R-1/U-2. Two variants of this tow plane were produced, one of which had conventional towing equipment (cable) and the other which had a rigid tow system developed by DFS. The H-16 also flew as a pathfinder aircraft once changes had been made to the radio equipment. Special-function gear was installed, similar to that of the H-15. The airplane was then designated the He 111 H-16/R-2. Approximately 1,100 H-16s were produced in 1943 alone. For the most part, they replaced the He 111 H-6 and H-11 in bomber units operating in the East. Delivery of the well-armed combat aircraft began in January 1943 and ended in early 1944. By 26 June 1944 the He 111, with its limited tactical performance, could only be found on the Eastern Front. In mid-1944 the following operational units flew various models of the Heinkel bomber in the following numbers:

- Stab KG 4 4
- I./KG 4 43
- I./KG 4 34
- III./KG 4 40
- Stab KG 27 1
- I./KG 27 41
- III./KG 27 35
- 14.(Eis)/KG 27 15
- Stab KG 53 1
- I./KG 53 36
- II./KG 5337
- III./KG 53 36
- Stab KG 55 1
- I./KG 55 35
- II./KG 5535
- III./KG 55 36
- 14.(Eis)/KG 55 9

In addition to the four Geschwader of the Luftwaffe equipped with the He 111 H, the Rumanian allies also flew the He 111 with a further two units — although these were earlier, obsolescent versions no longer needed by the Luftwaffe:

- Rumanian 22/1 Reconnaissance Sq. 8
- Rumanian IV Bomber Gp. 15

In the meantime, developments had shown that even the enemy on the Eastern Front had grown stronger not just in numbers, but also in tactical combat abilities. This had the result of making daylight attacks with the He 111 costly propositions — particularly if fighter protection wasn't available in strength. The development of a high-performance night bomber based on the He 111 H-16 was called for.

Therefore, initial tests were conducted using three prototypes, the He 111 V46, V47 and V48, all having reduced defensive armament. The goal was to develop a night bomber which was to later carry the designation **He 111 H-18**. This was most certainly to be based on the modification of the already existing H-6 and H-16 versions of the bomber and their variants. On the H-18 the nose gun position was fitted with an MG FF, the dorsal gun was an MG 131 B2 and the ventral gun an MG 81Z. Side gun positions were dropped for weight reasons and because for a time they were considered unnecessary for night missions. The new version — which as a rule only had a crew of three — could carry a bomb load of up to 2,000 kg to a range of 2,800 km. After testing had been completed some of the new models were delivered to Kommando Rastedter in Bordeaux fitted with a new type of exhaust flame damper as replacements for the H-4 and H-14. In addition, production aircraft differed from the previously mentioned prototypes by utilizing improved armor protection. The 24 He 111 H-18s which were initially delivered with the sharply reduced weapons systems carried the Rüstsatz (factory modification set) designation of R-1, while the He 111 H-18/R-2 had its defensive armament increased to counter the enemy's tactical advantages. Due to their performance characteristics, most of these aircraft served on the Eastern Front.

The version known as the **He 111 H-19** was to have been an H-16 with wooden propellers. No further information is available on this type.

The next and final all-new production version which followed the He 111 H-16 was the **He 111 H-20**, of which over 600 examples were produced beginning in early 1944. This variant primarily served as a night bomber (H-20/R-1), some of which were modified as transport aircraft. Additional H-20s flew as the H-20/U-1 courier aircraft. This also applied to some He 111 H-20s which operated as transports on the Eastern Front with the designation of H-20/R-2. In addition to their use as combat transports, carrying up to 16 paratroopers and their supplies, these aircraft could also be employed as bombers at any time using bombing equipment taken from the He 111 H-11.

The He 111s of Transportgruppe (TGr.) 30 flew 765 missions between 12 April 1944 and 11 May 1944 alone, carrying 6,240 soldiers and 280,000 kg of supplies into the Crimea. A further 762 250-kilogram supply packages were dropped over the region in support of friendly troops. Working in conjunction with other Luftwaffe units, an additional 1,640 men and 12,480 wounded were flown out, with only six He 111s being lost to enemy action. The majority returned

Test-running the engines before takeoff.

from their sorties either lightly damaged or without a scratch altogether. Eventually the He 111s were transferred to the area of Lemberg-Krosno, which served as a base of operations for TGr. 30, along with the fully subordinated I/KG 40 and segments of Kampfgeschwader 54 and 55. Under the command of Transportfliegerführer 2, these units flew successful supply missions in support of the 1. Panzerarmee. Compared to the number of flights, losses were low, e.g. Transportgruppe 30 lost only two He 111s to the enemy, with an additional 14 returning to base damaged. Two crews were lost to pilot error. Thanks to air support, by the 10th of April 1944 the 1. Panzerarmee was able to break through to the main lines. Apart from the previously mentioned He 111 H-20 modifications, the He 111 H-20 was also produced as an entirely new design — primarily as a horizontal bomber. The bombing system permitted up to 20 50-kg , 9 250-kg, or 8 250-kg and one 500-kg bomb to be carried. Alternatively, the aircraft could be loaded at any time with four SC 500, three SC 1000, two SC 1400 or an SC 2500 bomb.

Shortly after introduction, the Umrüst (conversion set) numbers were changed to Rüstsatz numbers. An example of the change includes the He 111 H-20/R-1/U-3 now designated as the He 111 H-20/R-3, a bomber with external ETC racks for carrying two SC/SD 1000 bomb loads. The He 111 H-20/R-4 was another design, which carried two SC 50 bombs on outer rack and was used for armed reconnaissance and harassment missions in the enemy's rear areas.

The next modification of the He 111 was the **He 111 H-21**, which was to have reached an average operating altitude of 9,200 meters. Test beds were the He 111 V52 and V53. Both prototypes were fitted with the Jumo 211 F-2 inline engine and were series-produced He 111 H-20s. The first 22 of these modified aircraft could be delivered to the units even before the installation of production exhaust turbochargers, and since He 111 H-20 aircraft had been made use of, these had been retro-fitted with high-performance turbochargers. Only a relatively few examples of the H-21 series flew on a test basis with two Jumo 213 engines. The eventual plans called for the fitting of Jumo 213 E-1 engines. Used in conjunction with

He 111 H operating on the Eastern Front.

An He 111 H-3 ready for the next mission. Notice the adjustable window above the pilot's seat.

Crew from KG 27; the aircraft is an He 111 H-3 (WerkNr. 3345).

6N + CB, formerly of Stab KGr. 100, awaits a modification increasing its firepower.

This He 111 H-3 served with 3./Aufklärungsgruppe (7A +) minus window gun mounts and with a modified ventral gun position.

the Hirth 9-2281 high-altitude turbo supercharger the aircraft was expected to attain an altitude of 12,500 meters and higher. However, since the exhaust turbines were never delivered in any great numbers and numerous technical and delivery problems were encountered with the Jumo 213, the He 111 H-21 in its intended form was dropped. It was still planned to use the more-powerful Jumo 213 engines as late as the summer of 1944, although without success. Out of necessity, then, the he 111 H-21 was forced to make use of the Jumo 211 F-2 engines with turbocharger. Since these were only available in limited quantities, the anticipated boost in performance for this He 111 variant was never realized.

The last version developed and produced in any numbers as a bomber belonged to the **He 111 H-22** series. This variant hearkened back to the He 111 V42, an earlier H-11/R-3/U-2, which initially underwent thorough testing in Peenemünde. Other than as a carrier for the V1 (FZG 76 = Fi 103), this version was not utilized as a standard bomber. The aircraft were modified from existing stocks of He 111 H-16 and H-20 in Oschatz and Grossenhain. In addition to re-equipping the bombers with suitable PVC 1006 bomb racks, fittings were installed for the V1 and parts of the vertical and horizontal stabilizers were fitted with steel plating to make them resistant to the exhaust heat. The majority of the aircraft thus modified flew with II./KG 53, later to become I./KG 53, beginning on 7 July 1944. Crews took off from Bramsche, Jever and Rheine and carried the V-1s to their intended targets on a route which took them over the North Sea. Aircraft took off at intervals of just 20 seconds and flew at an altitude of only 90 meters. 100 to 150 km before the target, speed was increased from 275 kmh to 350 kmh and the aircraft climbed to 400 m altitude. Prior to this, the V1 engines were electrically pre-heated. After the pulse engine was ignited the missile had to be held on the ETC rack for ten seconds before releasing. Because of the engine exhaust the carrier aircraft was illuminated so brightly that it could be seen for a distance of 25 km. British Mosquito long-range fighters and numerous accidents resulted in the loss of nearly 80 of these aircraft. Some of these crashed when the missile exploded while still attached to the plane. When attached, the V1 caused the He 111 H-22 a loss in speed of approximately 20 kmh.

British countermeasures and the ever-increasing fuel shortage eventually spelled an end for the night-time missions with the V1. The remaining inventory (quite a low number) of these modified He 111s were transferred from northern Germany to Luftflotte 6 on the Eastern Front.

Probably the last version of the Heinkel bomber to actually be completed was the **He 111 H-23**. This was another specialized variant and modification of the He 111 H-20 which was used to insert small groups (up to eight men and two supply packets) by night into enemy territory. Since a large quantity of other aircraft — some of even Allied origin — were available to KG 200 for paradropping agents, the majority of H-23s were converted back to bombers.

In addition to being used as a bomber on the Eastern Front, supply operations were also carried out to Kovel (March-April 1944), the 1. Panzerarmee and in April 1944 at Tarnopol. In July of 1944 towed gliders brought supplies to the endangered 12. Panzerdivision.

On 10 January 1945 the operational readiness report of the Luftwaffe noted the following He 111 units and their strength:

- Stab KG 4 1
- I./KG 4 25
- II./KG 4 23
- III./KG 4 24
- IV./KG 4 14
- Stab KG 53 1
- I./KG 53 37
- II./KG 5333
- III./KG 53 30
- IV./KG 53 14

Additionally, the He 111 could be found serving with many smaller units. Loss reports from January and February 1945 showed that the following He 111 units were operating with Luftflotte 6 alone:

- Fliegerverbindungsgeschwader 2
- Frontwetterstaffel Luftflotte 3
- IV./Transportgeschwader 4
- Transportgruppe 30 (TGr. 30)
- I. and III./Kampfgeschwader 4 (KG 4)
- 14. (Eisenbahnbekämpfungsstaffel)/KG 27
- II./Kampfgeschwader 53 (KG 53)
- 14. (Eisenbahnbekämpfungsstaffel)/KG 55
- I./Kampfgeschwader 200 (KG 200)
- Kurierstaffel des Oberkommandos des Heeres (OKH)
- Schleppergruppe 1
- Stab Nahaufklärungsgruppe 3 (NAG 3)

The last two large-scale operations in which the He 111 participated in numbers took place shortly before the end of the war with supply missions to the beleaguered "fortresses" of Budapest and Breslau. Between 28 December 1944 and 15 February 1945 the pocket of Budapest was supplied by Ju 52s (III./TG 2 and III./TG 3), Do 17s and Ju 87s (I./LLG 2) and He 111s towing DFS 230 gliders. In addition, food and other supplies were dropped in canisters by He 111 Hs of KG 4 (Major Graubner). During the final night of operations, on 15 February 1945, three Ju 52s and nine He 111s were used. The air supply missions were canceled on 16 February due to the hopelessness of the situation and the He 111s were transferred to Dresden-Klotsche along with the remaining Ju 52s. Eventually these saw service over Breslau, Glogau, Graudenz and Posen. 60 He 111 Hs were listed as available for one of the first missions there. In order to reach the surrounded troops in bad weather, by night, and even in blind-flying conditions, on 27 February 1945 a directive was given to fit the airplanes with the FuG 200 and FuG 225 "Biene" identification equipment, beginning with a Staffel of KG 4. Fuel shortages forced the disbandment in March of 1945 of two units participating in resupply operations, the III./KG 53 and the 14./(Eis)/KG 55. An example of these operations took place on 22 March 1945, when a total of 22 He 111s from KG 4

An He 111 H-3 of KG 100 with low-visibility midnight black paint scheme.

The H-3 was the first version to have a fixed MG 17 installed in the tail.

An He 111 H-3 of KG 27 on the Eastern Front.

dropped 104 food containers in succession into the "Fortress Breslau", surrounded by the Red Army. One of the three Go 242s towed into the target area was shot down by Soviet anti-aircraft fire, and one out of the three DFS 230s also crashed. Over "Fortress Glogau" crews of 13 He 111 Hs dropped a further 72 supply canisters with 12,100 kg of ammunition. In April 1945 Lufthansa Ju 52s and two He 111 Staffeln of III./KG 4 were pressed into service for supply operations and flew these missions in the East right up until the last few days of the war

As long as fuel and replacement parts held out, transportation and supply missions were the primary roles shortly before the war's end for units still equipped with the He 111 — some of which only had a handful of aircraft. The last known He 111 mission took place in support of "Fortress Breslau" on 27 April 1945 and delivered 24, 120 kg of supplies into the combat zone.

By 9 April 1945 there were no more He 111s within the Luftflotte Reich's district, other than a small number still operating with KG 200. For Luftflotte 6 there were barely 30 airplanes operationally serviceable, pieced together from the remnants of the two Kampfgeschwader, KG 4 and KG 53:

- Stab KG 4	1
- I./KG 4	27
- 8./KG 4	4
- 7./KG 53	4

Two tow- and transportation Gruppen were formed from the remaining inventory of He 111s.

KGr. 100 operations in the East; depicted is one of the unit's He 111 H-3s.

Above: preparing for a combat mission in Russia.

Center: Loading an He 111 H-5 with the aid of a bomb-lifting pole. This bomb load is being carried in four internal ESAC containers and on one external PVC 1006 rack.

Below: Bomb hits during an attack on a transport convoy in the rear area.

These were operated as tugs for Go 242s and DFS 230s by "Gruppe Uhl" from Rerik on the Baltic Sea (east of Wismar) and by "Gruppe Herzog" in Hohenmauth (northeast of Prague) on 30 April 1945 to supply Berlin and Breslau. Eventually, parts of "Gruppe Uhl" pulled back to Eggebeck in Holstein on 4 May 1945.

Approximately 5,656 He 111 airplanes were built from 1939 and the time production stopped. Altogether, a total of 7,000 aircraft of all variants was produced. From 1935 to 31 December 1941 more than 2,000 of Heinkel's bomber left the plant. In 1942 alone 1,337 were produced, and in the following year the figure rose to 1,405. Copies of the He 111 were made by Arado in Brandenburg, Dornier in Wismar, Junkers in Schersieben, as well as by ATG in Leipzig.

Once the war was over, the victors found just 274 destroyed He 111s when they did an inventory of captured material; another 12 were in Denmark and four in Norway. Hardly a sing aircraft was still serviceable. Only in Eggesbeck were there roughly ten He 111s of various types which had probably belonged to Gruppe Uhl. As far as the Western Allies were concerned, these aircraft weren't even worth the effort of carting them off as war prizes.

However, in Czechoslovakia some of the He 111s (under the designation LB 77) left behind by the Luftwaffe were converted to passenger airliners or bombers and continued to be flown for several years.

Many He 111s were captured in the former USSR during the war in more or less flyable condition. the fuselage of 1T + KX was put on display in the streets of Moscow in the late autumn of 1941. Another He 111 (1H + AK), from KG 26, fell into the hands of the Red Army near Kalinin on 17 December 1941. Additionally, an He 111 with Jumo 211 F-1 engines was test flown by the NII VVS testing facility. The aircraft was later used as a tow tug for the Antonov An-7 transport glider and pressed into service carrying supplies to those partisan groups operating in the Baltic. On 25 March 1943 an He 111 H-6 and H-11 were flight tested by the NII-VVS and later put on display in Moscow. A Slovakian He 111 H-10 (WerkNr. 5313) was captured on 2 August 1944, followed by WerkNr. 701678 on 7 Feb 1945.

At least two He 111s were tested by the RAF during the war. A third aircraft accidentally landed at an RAF airfield on 14 February 1942. The crew discovered their error in time and took off again. There

The He 111 H-4 was equipped with either internal bomb racks or two external PVC 1006 racks for heavy ordnance, as seen here.

This He 111 H-3 belonged to II./KG 27. The machine in the foreground is a starting cart.

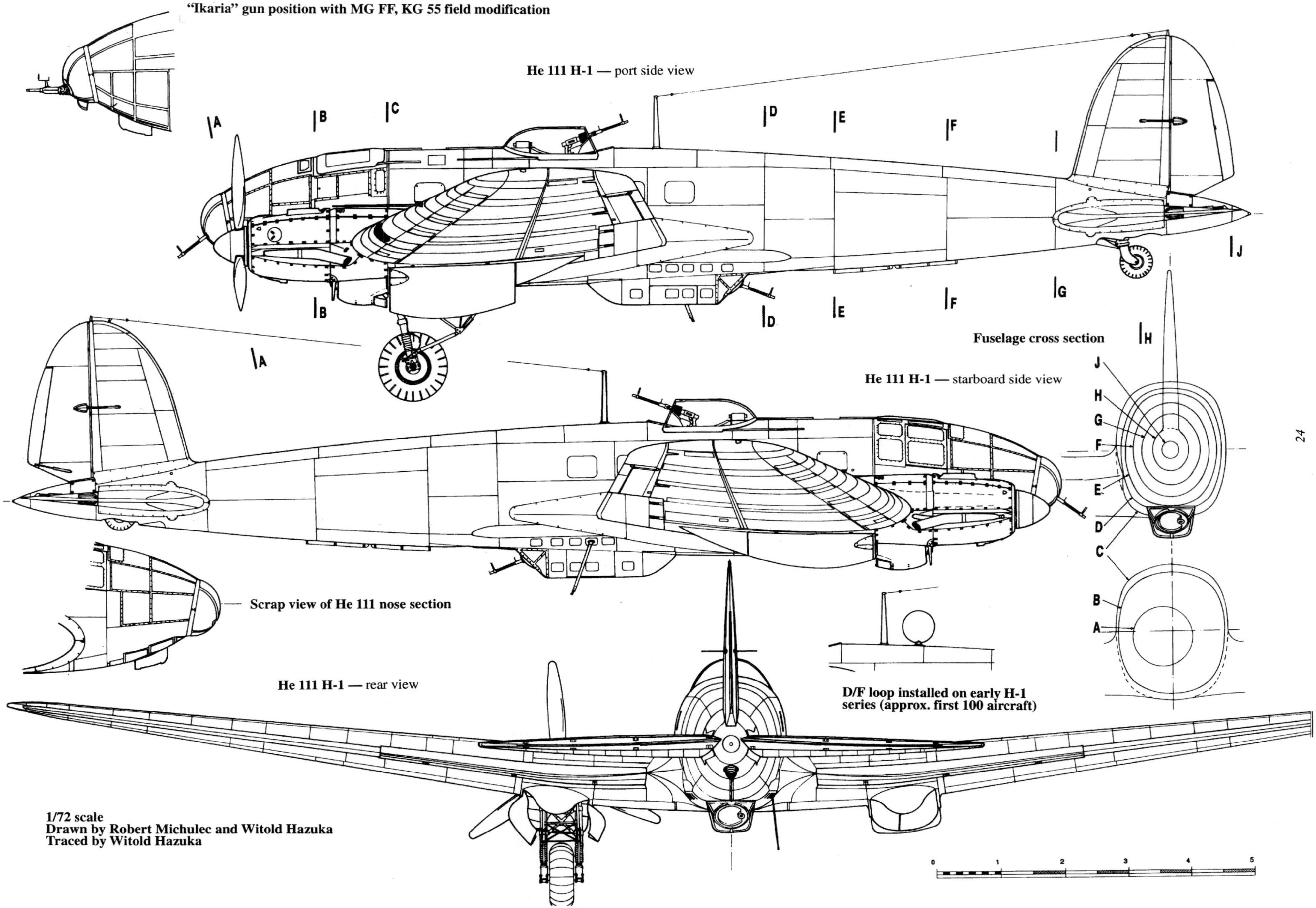

"Ikaria" gun position with MG FF, KG 55 field modification

He 111 H-1 — port side view

He 111 H-1 — starboard side view

Fuselage cross section

Scrap view of He 111 nose section

He 111 H-1 — rear view

D/F loop installed on early H-1 series (approx. first 100 aircraft)

1/72 scale
Drawn by Robert Michulec and Witold Hazuka
Traced by Witold Hazuka

Drawn by Robert Michulec and
Witold Hazuka
Traced by Witold Hazuka

1/72 scale

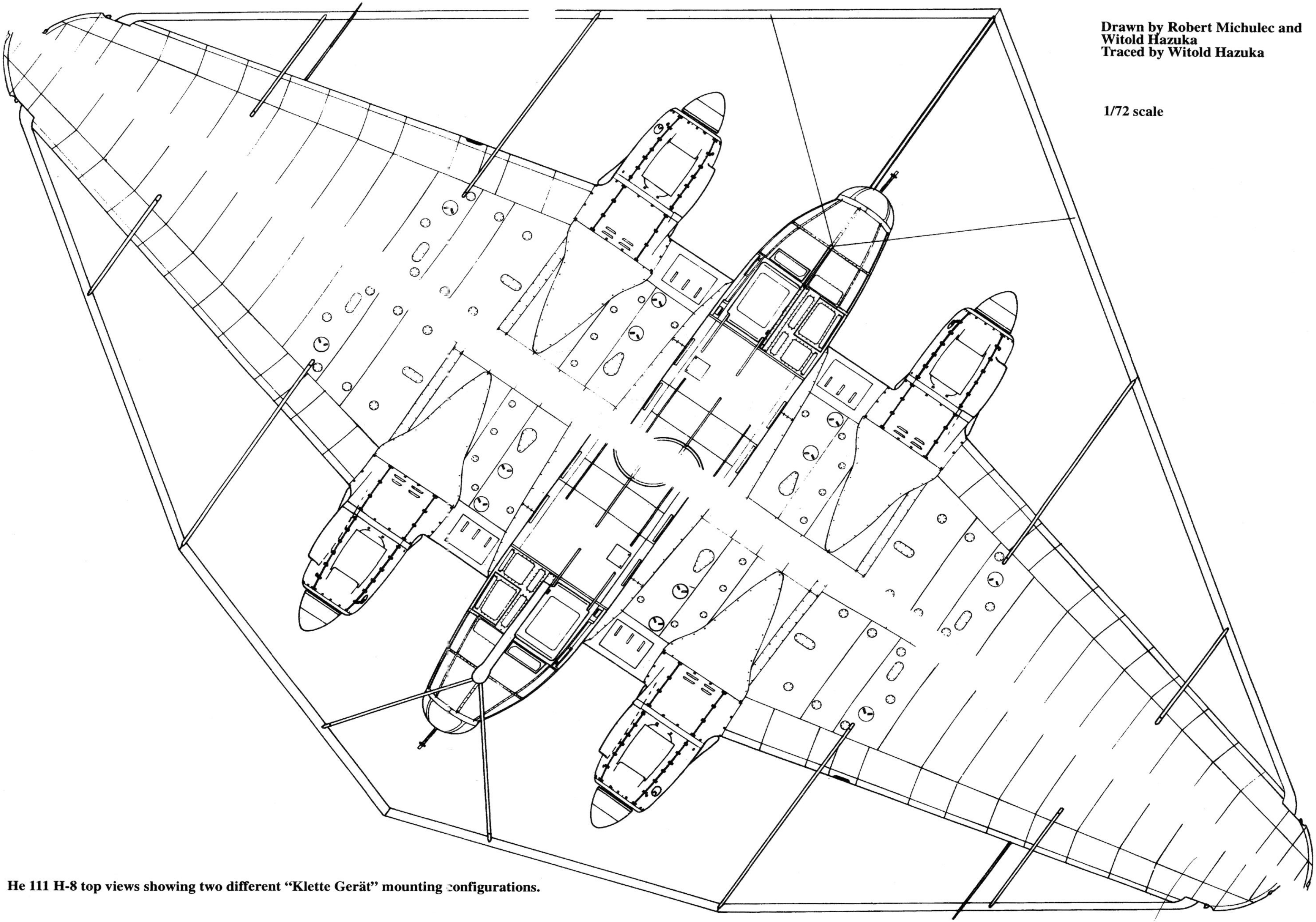

He 111 H-8 top views showing two different "Klette Gerät" mounting configurations.

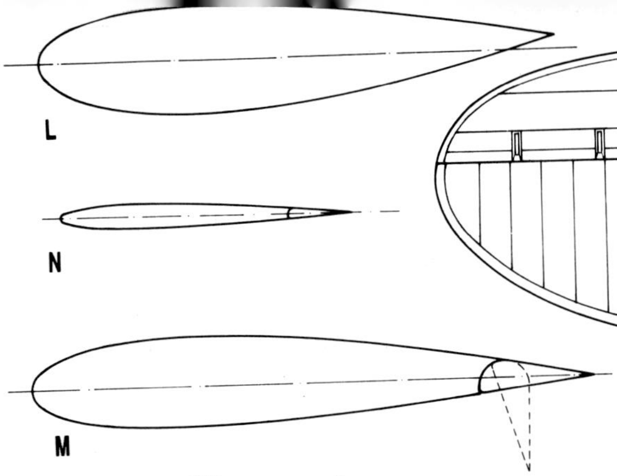

Wing cross section

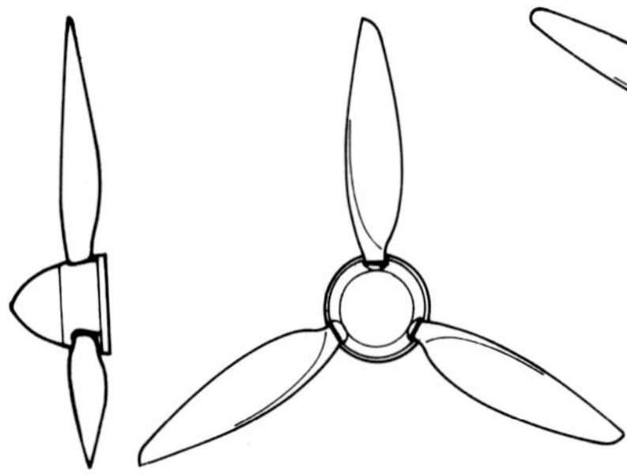

Junkers VS 11 wooden propeller used on H-6 and later variants.

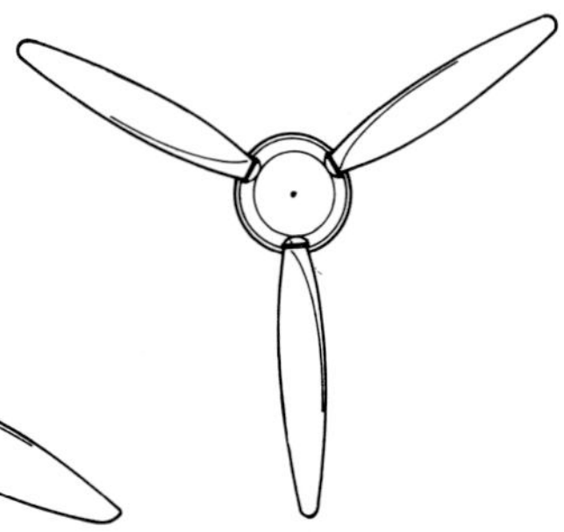

VDM metal propeller used on H-5 and earlier variants.

He 111 H-1 – top view

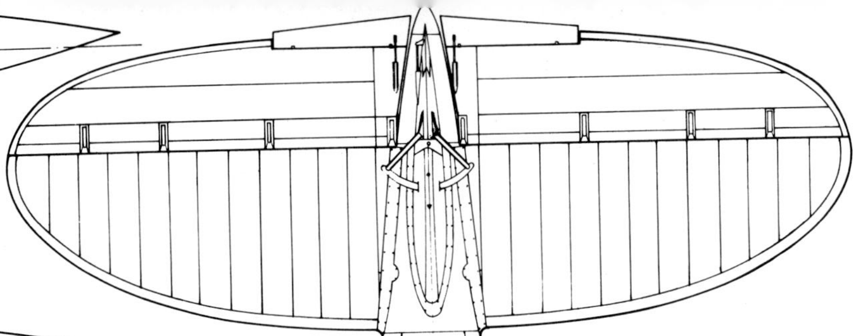
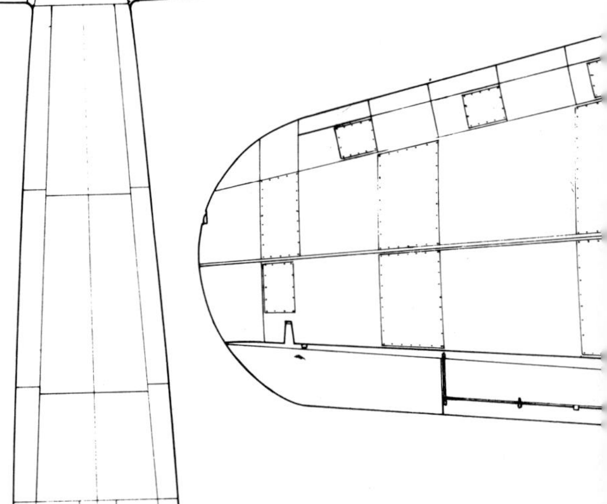
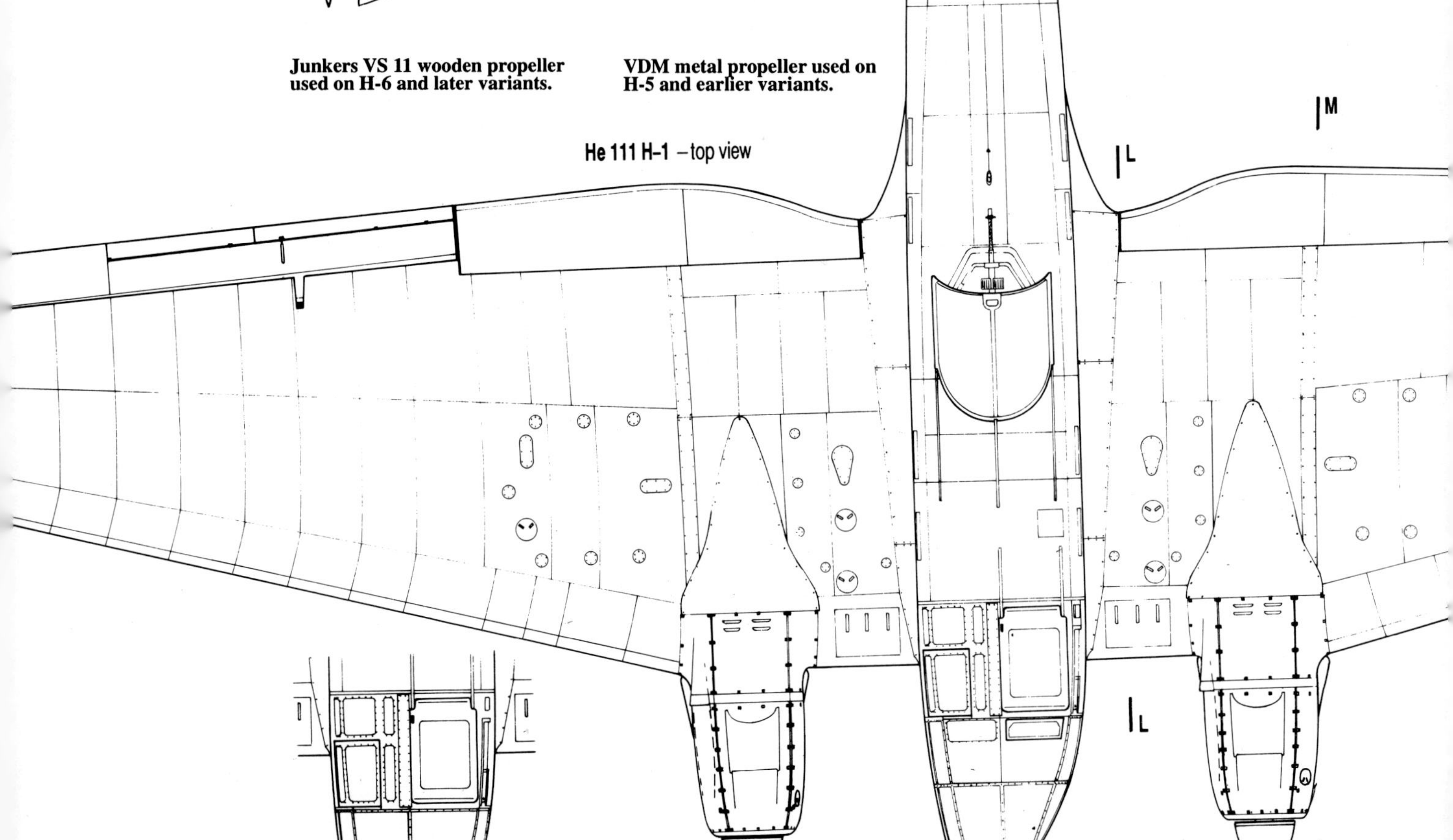

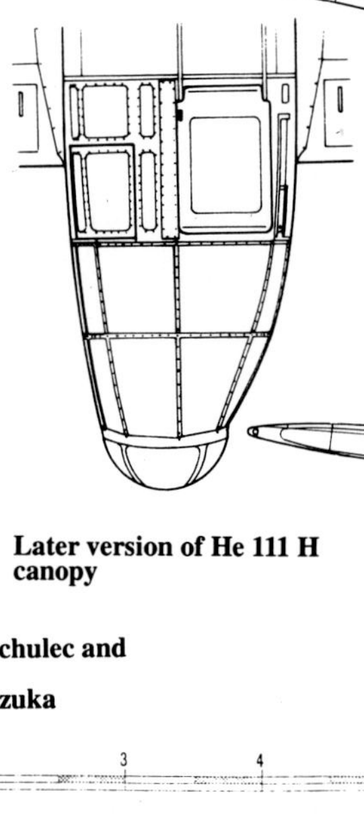

Later version of He 111 H canopy

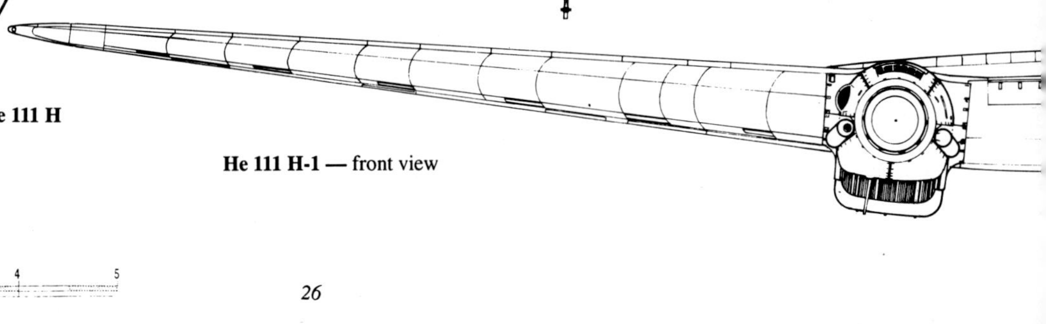

He 111 H-1 — front view

1/72 scale

Drawn by Robert Michulec and Witold Hazuka
Traced by Witold Hazuka

He 111 H-1 — bottom view

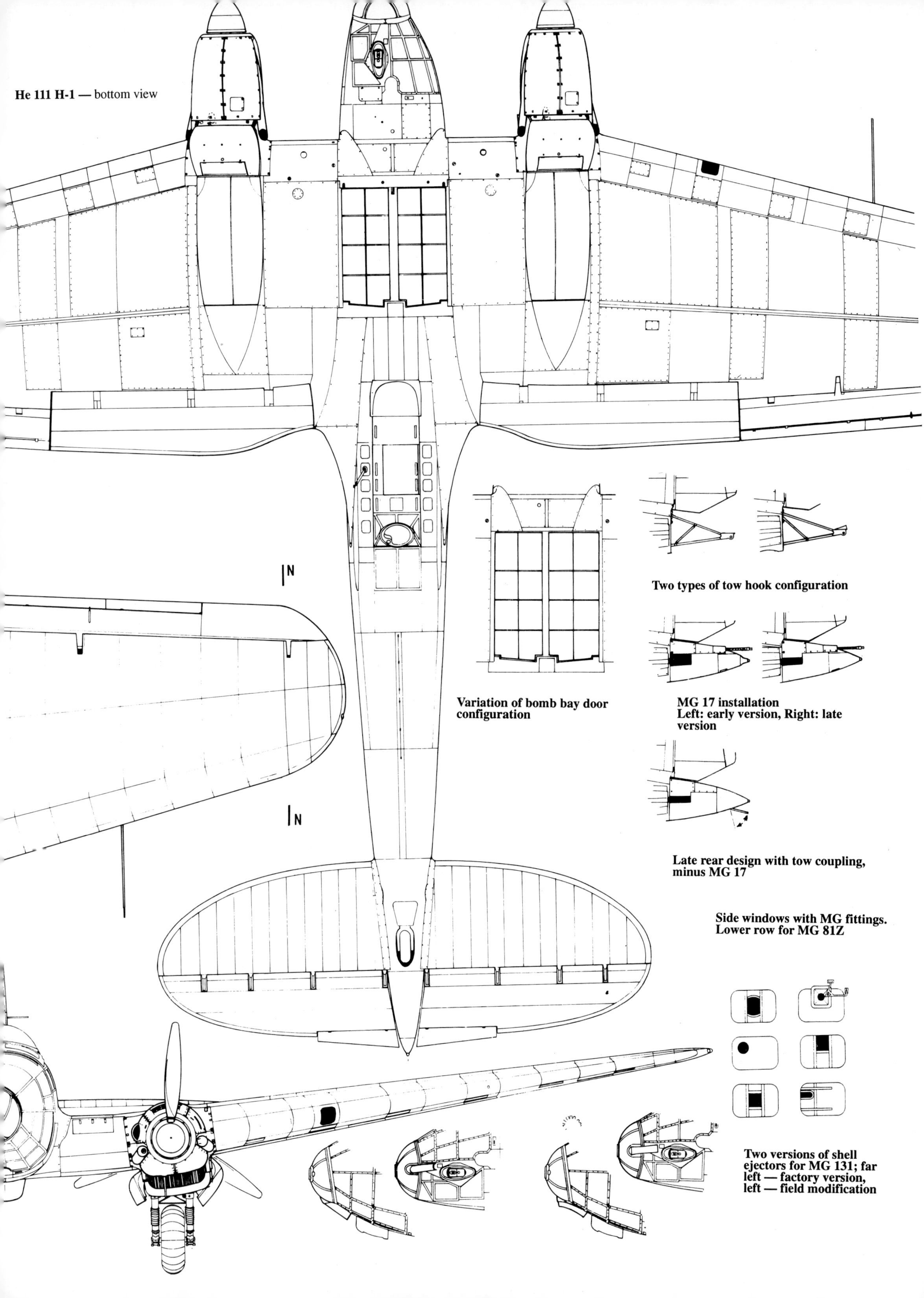

Variation of bomb bay door configuration

Two types of tow hook configuration

MG 17 installation
Left: early version, Right: late version

Late rear design with tow coupling, minus MG 17

Side windows with MG fittings. Lower row for MG 81Z

Two versions of shell ejectors for MG 131; far left — factory version, left — field modification

VIP transport version of the **He 111 H** and **P**

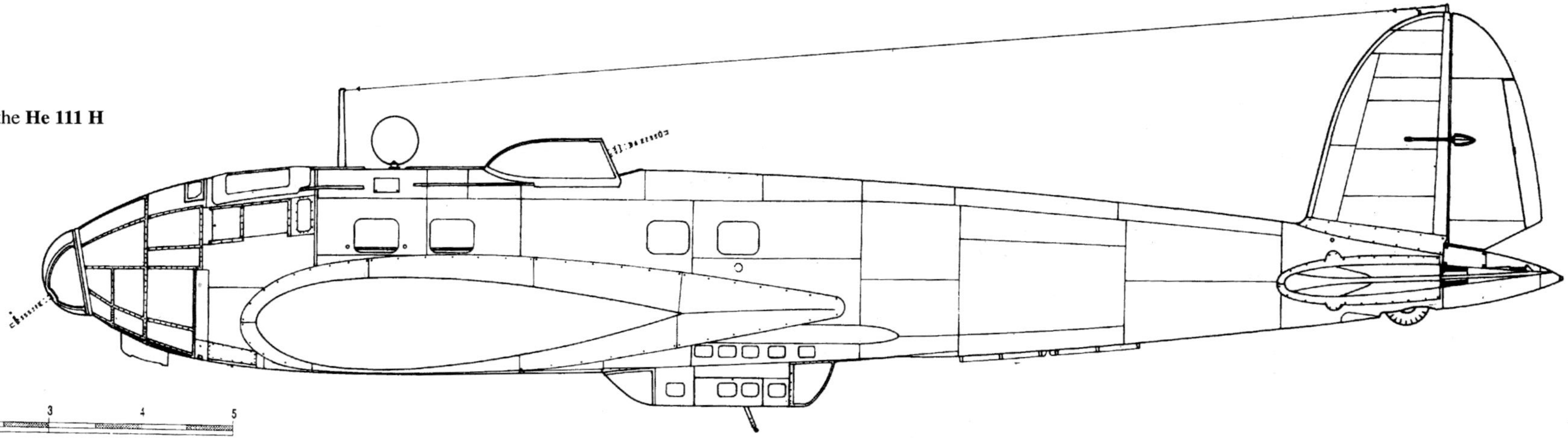

1/72 scale

Dorsal gunner station on the **H-3** to **H-5**, latter half of 1940

He 111 H-3

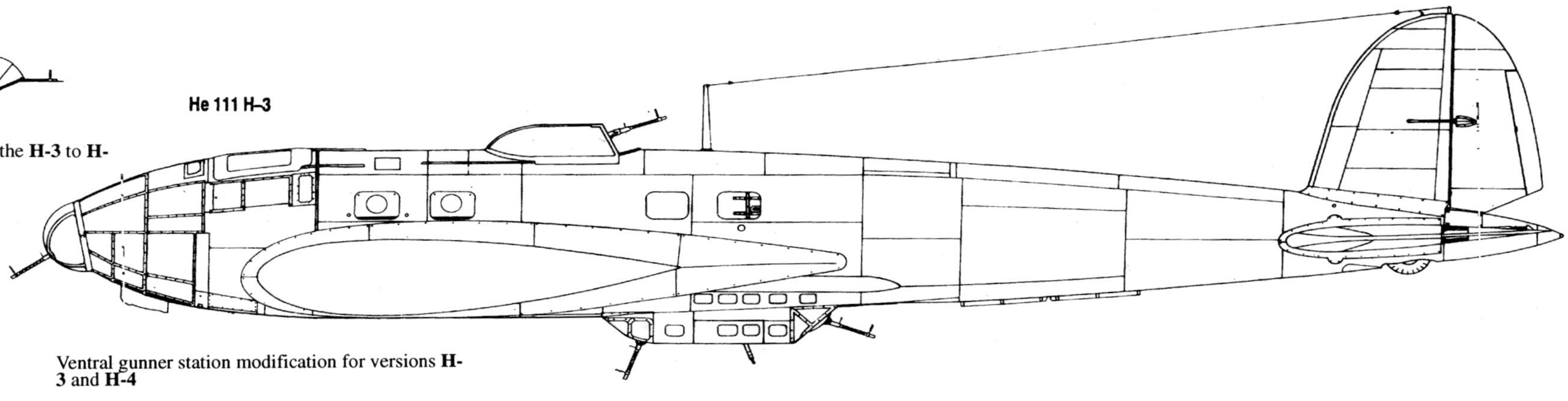

Ventral gunner station modification for versions **H-3** and **H-4**

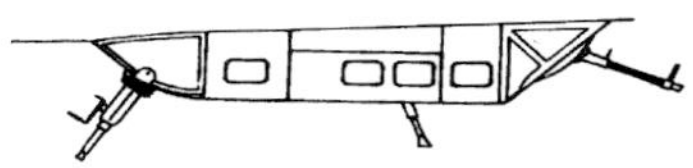

He 111 H-4 with PVC racks

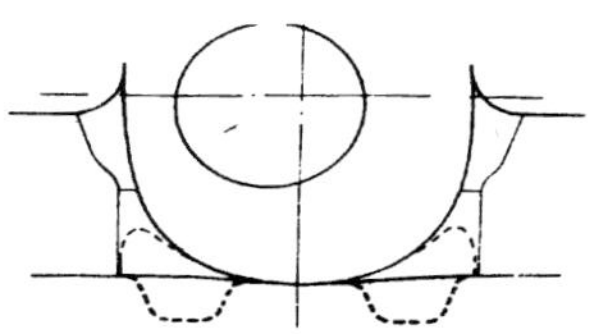

Front view showing positioning of PVC racks

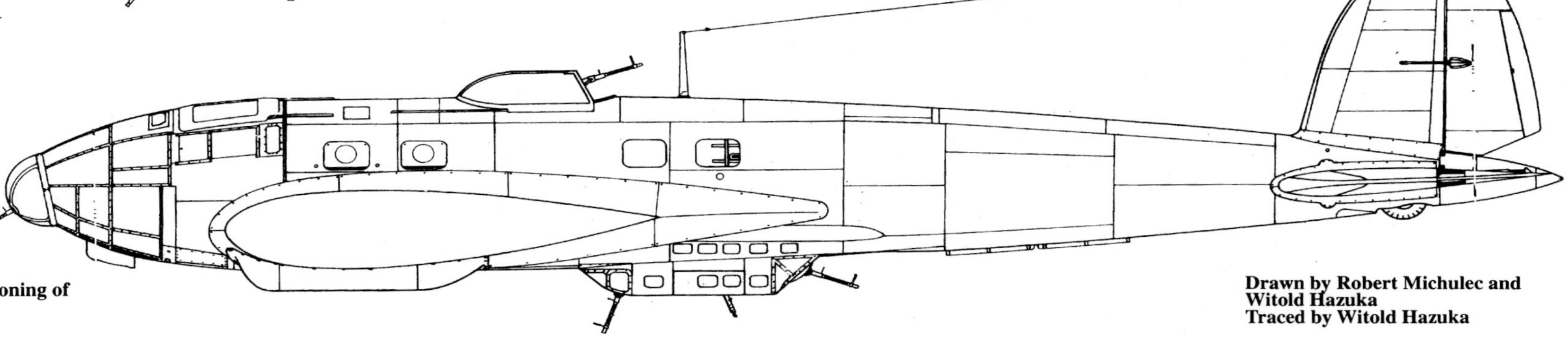

Drawn by Robert Michulec and Witold Hazuka
Traced by Witold Hazuka

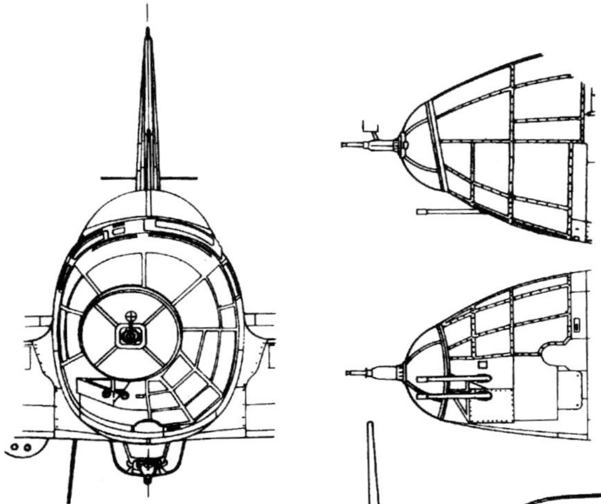

Scrap three-view of air/ground attack variant with four additional guns

MG 15 installations. Left: field modification, Right: production version

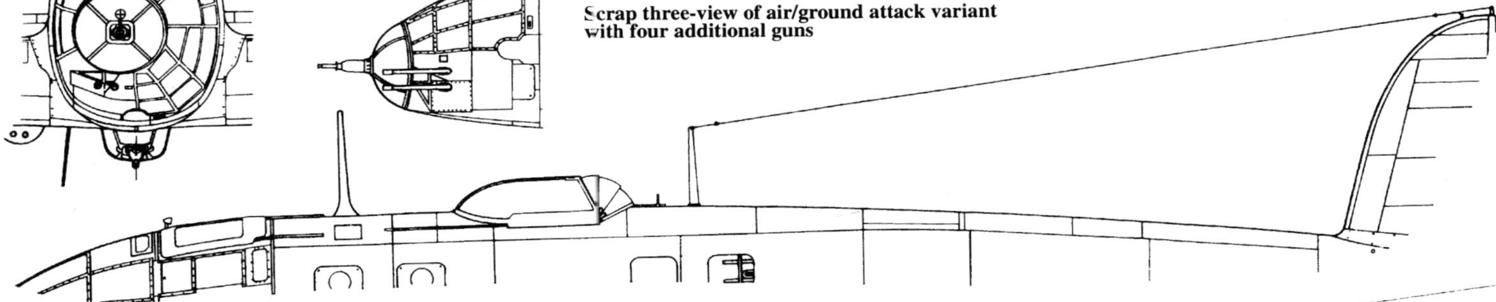

He 111 H-5y with "Y-Gerät"

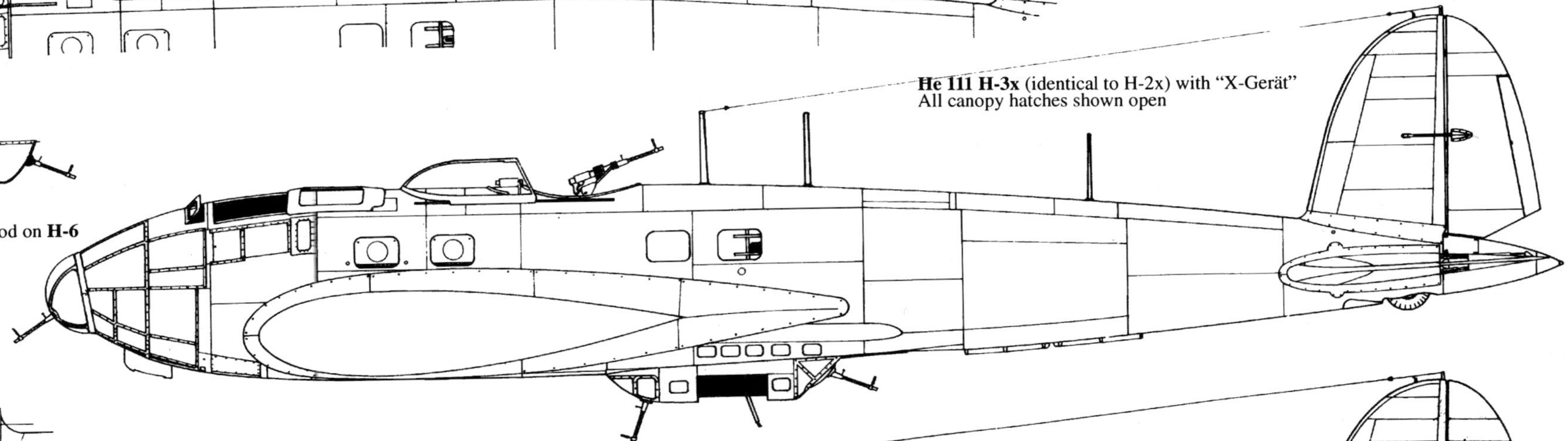

He 111 H-3x (identical to H-2x) with "X-Gerät"
All canopy hatches shown open

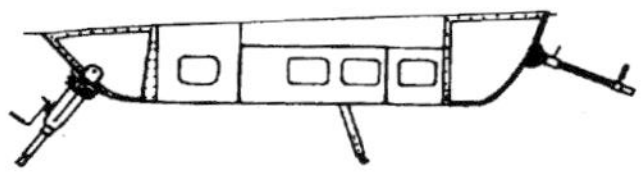

Modification of ventral pod on **H-6**

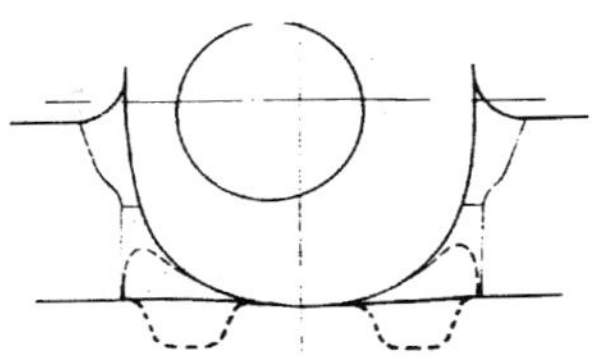

Position of PVC racks on **H-6**

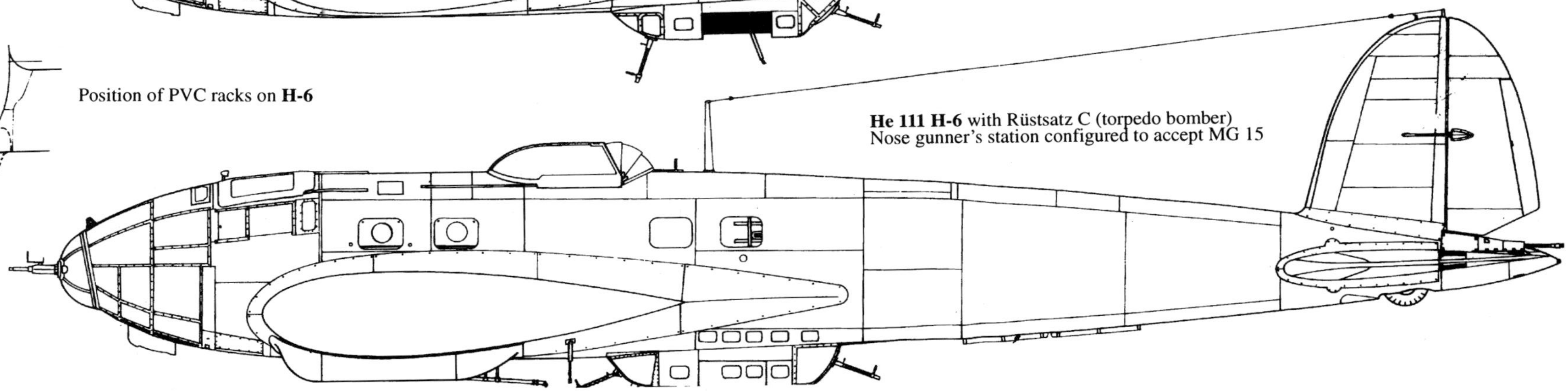

He 111 H-6 with Rüstsatz C (torpedo bomber)
Nose gunner's station configured to accept MG 15

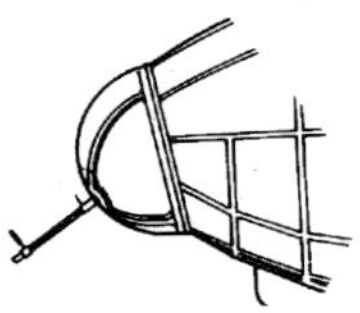

Early H-6 with Ikaria turret

1/72 scale
Drawn by Robert Michulec and Witold Hazuka

He 111 H-12 and **H-15**, early platforms for V-1 flying bombs

Drawn by Robert Michulec and Witold Hazuka
Traced by Witold Hazuka

1/72 scale

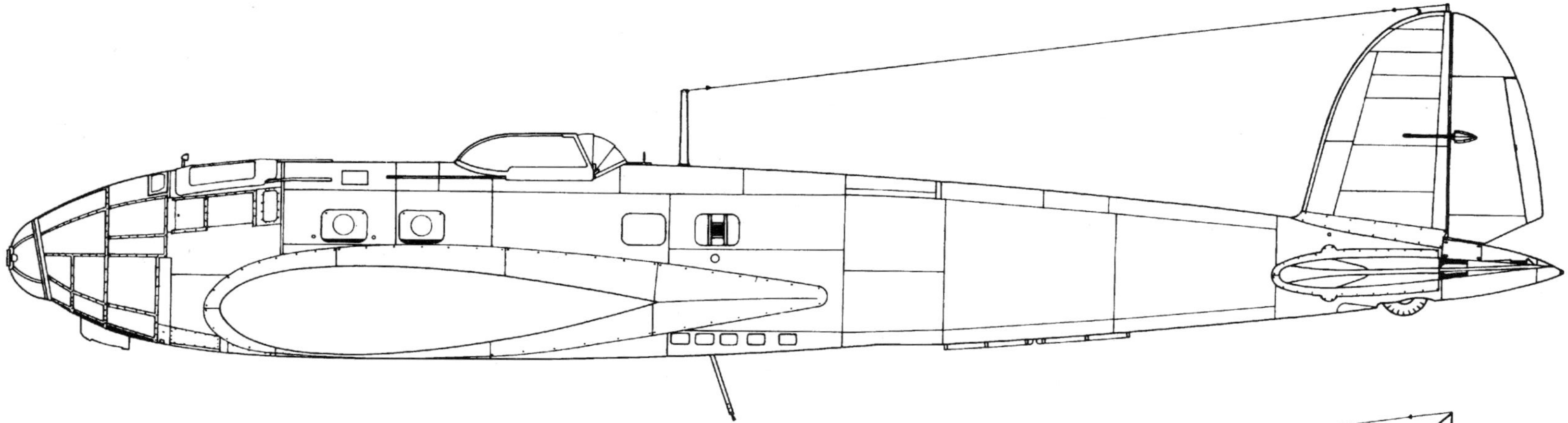

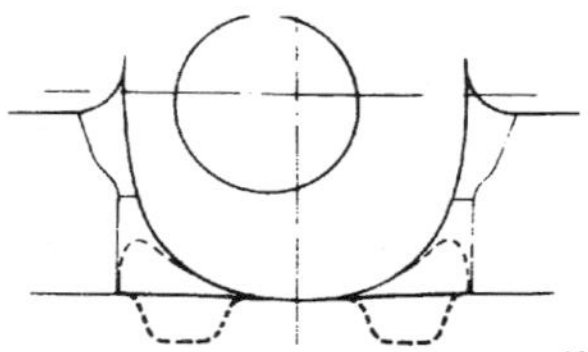

Position of PVC racks on **H-16** variants

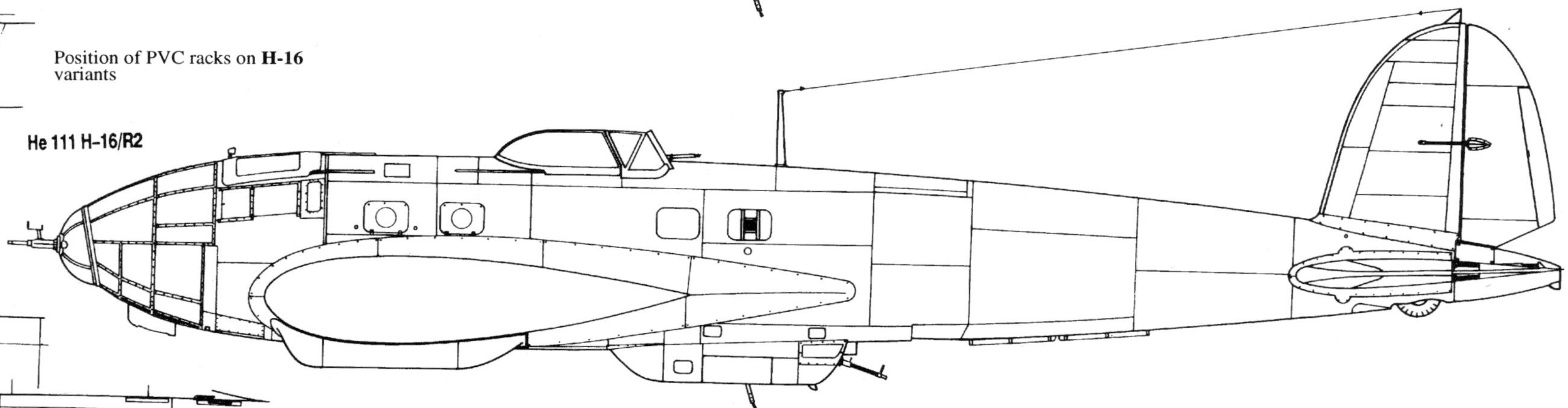

Position of the FuG 16 antenna

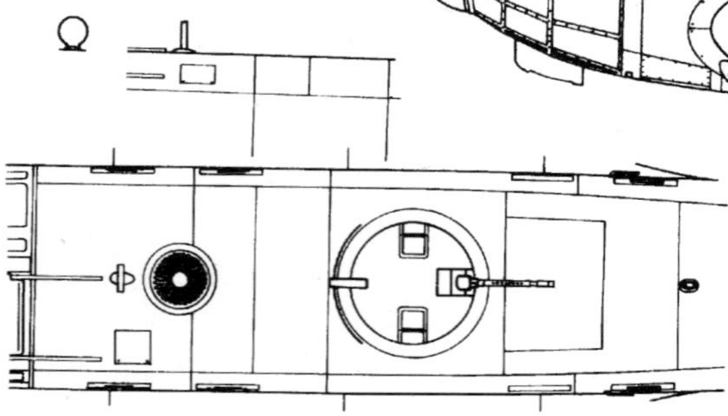

Scrap top view of **H-20** fuselage center section

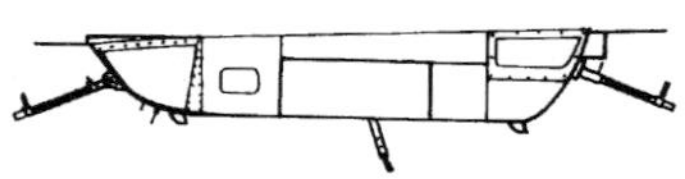

Modification of ventral pod on **H-16**

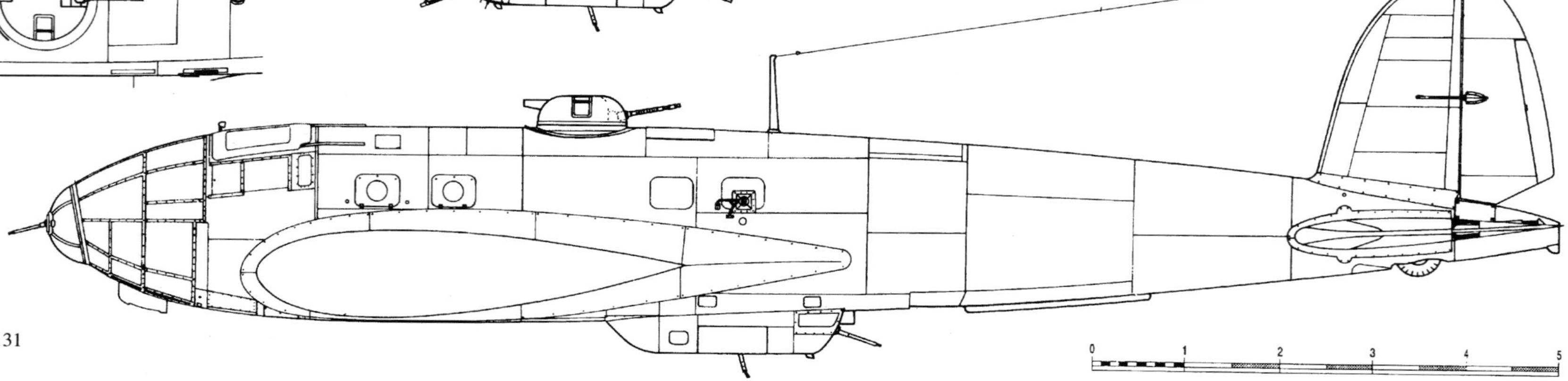

He 111 H-20/R-2 with MG 131 in nose and side window mounts for MG 81Z

Heinkel He 111 H-6 with Rüstsatz C, KG 26

Heinkel He 111 H-22 with V-1 (Fi 103) flying bomb

Drawings: **Hawk**
Copyright: Flugzeug Publikations GmbH

Color scheme: standard scheme of RLM 71 Dunkelgrün with splinter RLM 70 Schwarzgrün.
Lower surfaces RLM 65 Hellblau.

Heinkel He 111 H-1. Although the 2H+ code doesn't indicate KG 26, the Geschwader emblem reveals the aircraft does indeed belong to this unit.

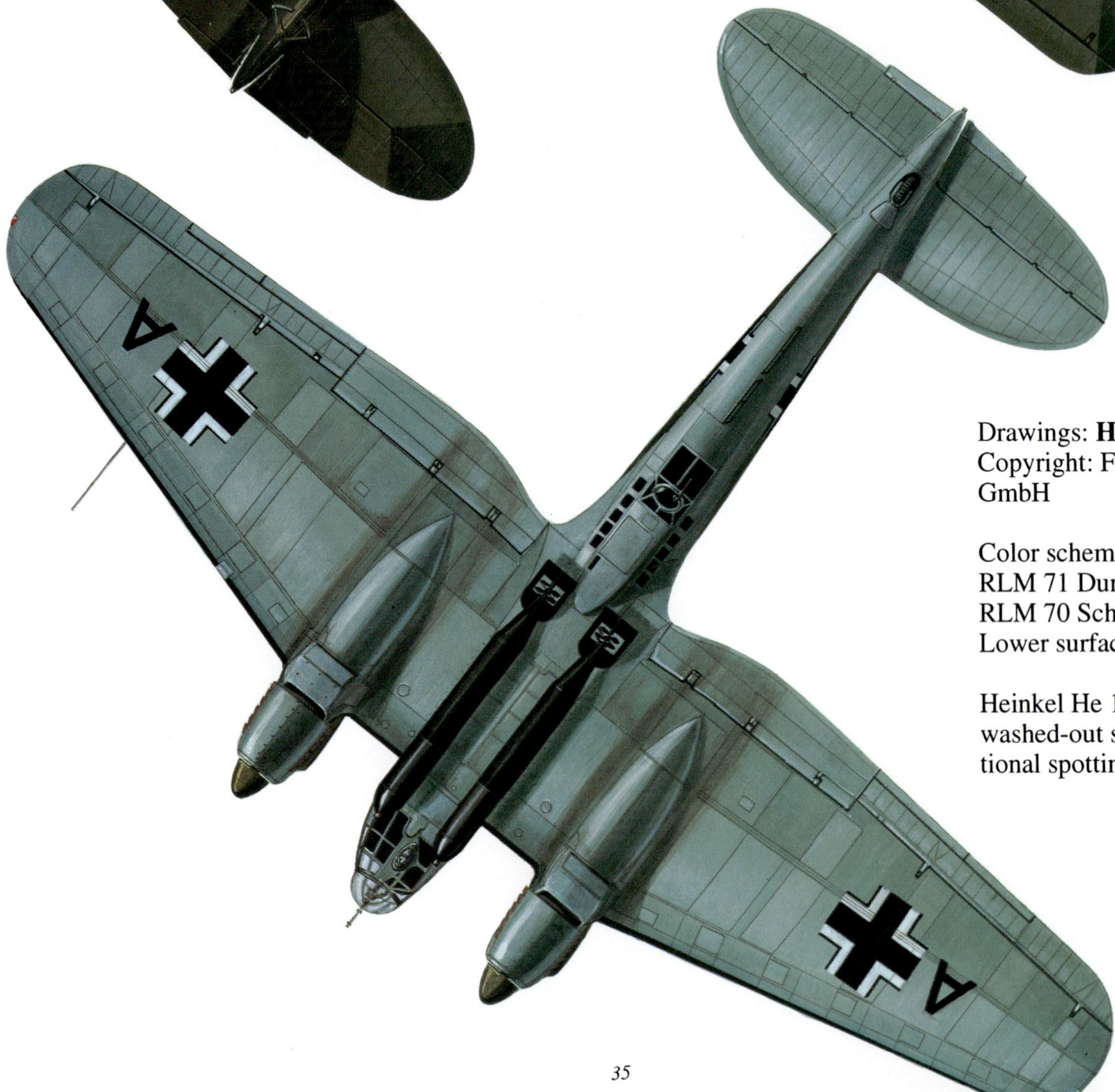

Drawings: **Hawk**
Copyright: Flugzeug Publikations GmbH

Color scheme: standard scheme of RLM 71 Dunkelgrün with splinter RLM 70 Schwarzgrün.
Lower surfaces RLM 65 Hellblau.

Heinkel He 111 H-22 (right) with washed-out standard scheme, additional spotting of RLM 76 Grau.

An He 111 H of III./KG 53 with exhaust flame dampers and black-painted underside.

This He 111 H-3 (WerkNr. 3325) flew with I. Gruppe of KG 100 in 1941.

Compensating an He 111 H-5 at the Oranienburg factory. Two Luftwaffe He 116s are in the background.

This photo of 6N + HK, an H-3, was taken at KGr. 100.

An He 111 H-4 on final approach in Rostock-Marienehe.

He 111 H-4 test flight operations at the Oranienburg factory. Notice the openings in the nose canopy for two MG 15s.

Recovering a crashed aircraft in the East.

were two other similar incidents that same night, but none of the He 111s were able to be captured. The first He 111 to be forced down by an RAF Spitfire Mk. 1 belonged to 5./KG 26 and carried the WerkNr. 6853, indicating that it was an H-3. The radio operator was killed in the duel with the Spitfire and the remainder of the crew was taken prisoner upon landing. The aircraft crashed at Polebrook on 10 November 1943 while being evaluated; the British pilot, Flying Officer F. A. Barr and his six-man crew were all killed in the resulting fire. The second He 111 to be flown in England was an H-23 (WerkNr. 701152, NT + FL) and was captured by the Americans, who turned it over to the British. The airplane was kept until 1976 in St. Athan and can now be admired in the "Battle of Britain" Museum at RAF Hendon. In Spain, 216 He 111 H-16s were license-built by CASA as the CASA 2.111, with production continuing until well after the war. As the supply of German aircraft engines became less and less, the aircraft were increasingly fitted with Rolls-Royce Merlin 500-20 engines. Some of these aircraft can be found today in various museums, such as the Deutsches Museum in Munich, the Luftwaffenmuseum in Uetersen, the Frankfurter Rhein-Main airport and in Sinsheim near Heilbronn. Two Spanish CASA 2.111 are on display in Madrid and Tablada. A further aircraft is in North Weald, England and two are in Harlingen and Topeka, in the U.S.A. Many He 111s, some in original condition, are still waiting to be recovered and restored, such as the airplane lying in the Grovel Zee and fragments of He 111 H-3 (WerkNr. 2501, 1H + DN) in Sweden. Additionally, there is the fuselage of another He 111 H in the Moscow Army Museum.

View from the headquarters building in Bordeaux-Merignac, Easter 1941.

In preparing this book, I would like to express my particular thanks to Mr. Karl-Ernst Heinkel, whose documents were able to clear up many points with regard to the order of variants and overall production of the He 111. In addition, for making available their documents I would like to thank Messrs. Balke, Bekker, Borzutzki, Dabrowski, Dressel, Filley, Fossyth, Franzke, Götz, Heck, Hefner, Herwig, Dr. Hiller, Holzmann, Jayne, Dr. Kranzhoff, König, Dipl.-Ing. Kössler, Lang, Lange, Lutz jr., Mankau, Menke, Meyer, Midel, van Mol, Müller, Müller-Romminger, Neitzel, Nowarra (dec.), Ott, Petrick, Price, Radinger, Regel, Riediger, Rohrbach, Schliephake, Schmitt, Selinger, Sengfelder, Soppa and Trenkle.

Furthermore, my gratitude goes out to my colleagues in the Deutsches Aeroclub, the Deutsches Gesellschaft für Luft- und Raumfahrt, the Deutsches Museum in Munich, the Flughafen AG in Frankfurt/Main, the National Air and Space Museum in Washington, D.C., the Lehrsammlung des BWB, the Bundesarchiv in Freiburg, the Zentralbibliothek der Bundeswehr as well as for many private collections.

An He 111 H-5 of Kampfgeschwader 55, stationed on the Eastern Front.

This well-concealed aircraft of I./KG 27 was one of the few remaining He 111 H-4s remaining in the West at the beginning of 1941.

This He 111 H-6 was equipped with a C-127 (or variant) approach and homing receiver.

Two He 111 Hs wearing the paint scheme typical for missions over the Balkans.

Series production of the He 111 H-6.

This He 111 H-6 draped with camouflage netting operated in the southern sector of the Eastern Front.

Crash landing of an He 111 H-6 armed with an MG FF in the nose gunner's station.

In addition to the He 111 H-3 and H-4, the fixed rear-firing MG 17 in the tail was also fitted to many He 111 H-6s.

Above: Carrying an SC 1000, this He 111 H-6 of II./KG 54 is bound for its target in the Eastern Front's central sector, winter 1942.

Right: This He 111 H-6 was stationed in northern France in 1941.

Three He 111 H-16s during a transfer flight over southern Germany.

Waiting for the next mission, 2./KG 27 in the East.

An He 111 H-10 (or H-11) somewhere along the Eastern Front, 1942.

The He 111 H-18 was designed exclusively for the night bomber role; having 2 x 4 ESAC bomb racks it was incapable of carrying the heavier bombs.

He 111 H-8 aircraft with balloon deflectors operated over southern England for only a relatively short period of time.

Loading an He 111 H-6 with two practice torpedoes.

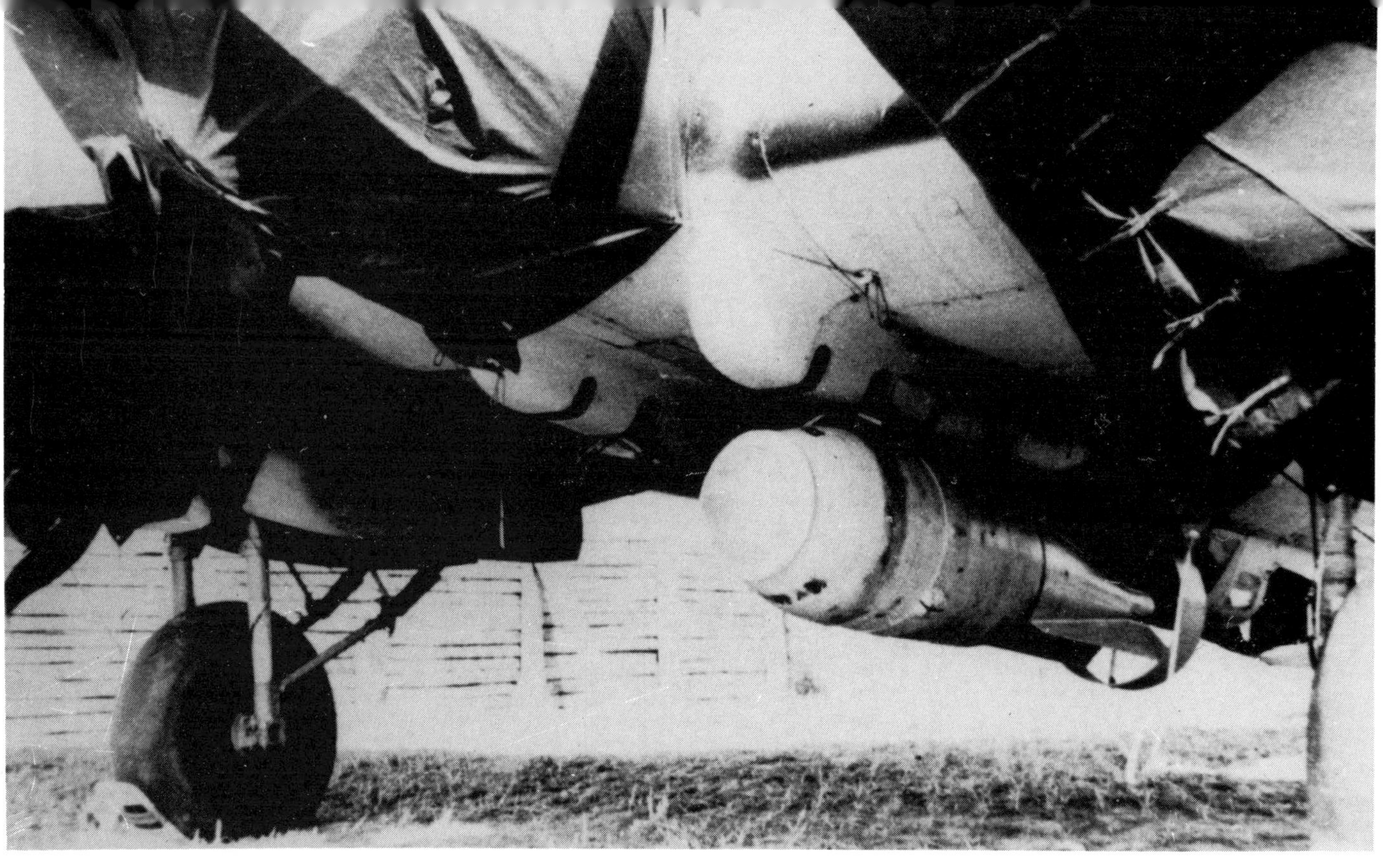

An He 111 H-4 loaded with an SC 1000 (slung beneath the PVC 1006 L).

Test flying at Heinkel; aircraft in the foreground is an He 111 H-11.

Above and below: This He 111 H-11 was fitted with an FuG 101 precision altimeter and a "Kutonase" for low-level attacks.

This He 111 H-6, with three underslung BV 246 "Hagelkorn" glide bombs, served as the forerunner of the planned He 111 H-15.

This He 111 H-11 returned from an operational sortie with its dorsal gunner's station shot to pieces.

The MG 81Z was first introduced on the He 111 H-11 as a replacement for the MG 15.

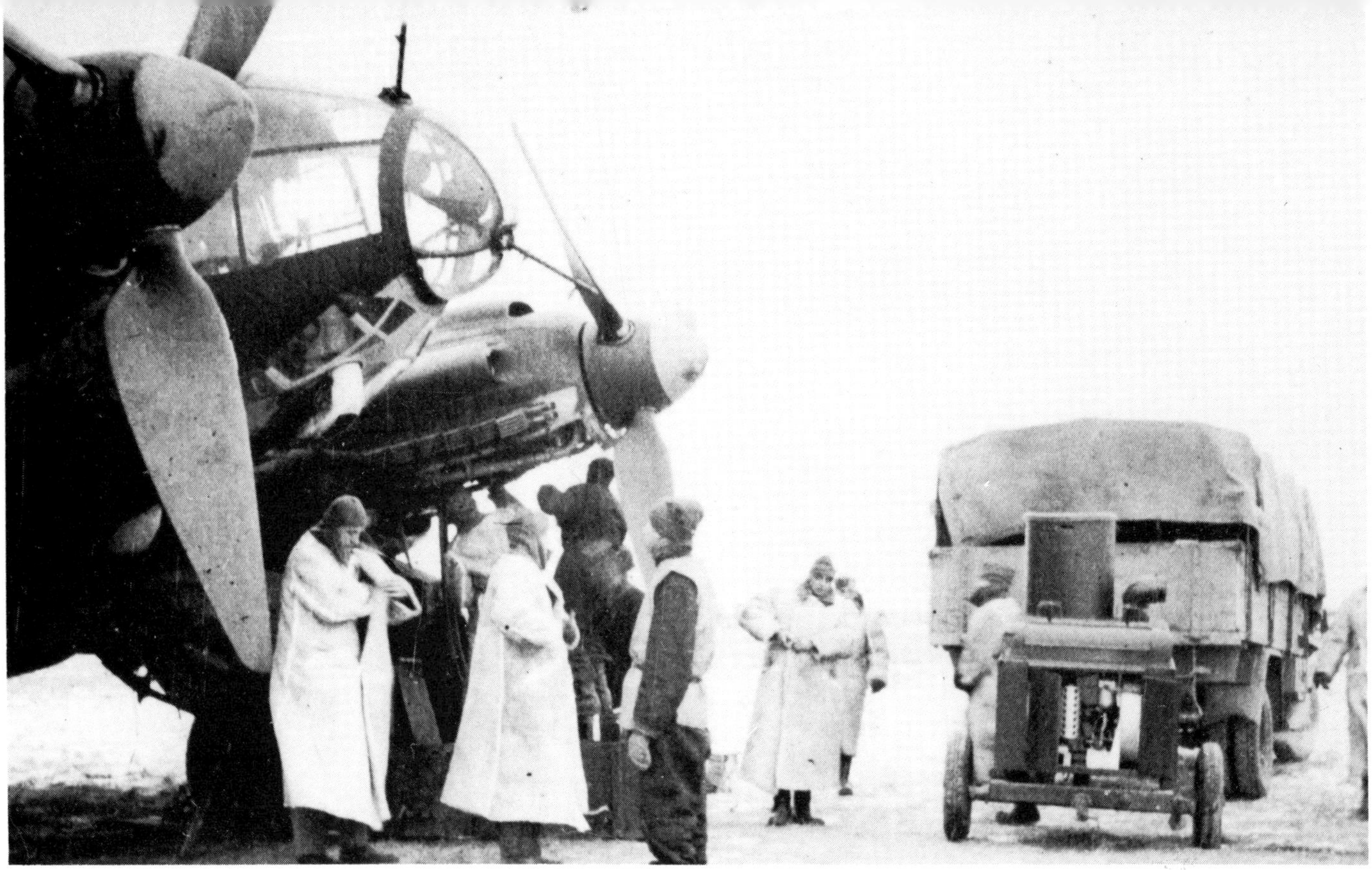

An He 111 H-6 of KGr. z.b.V. 1 (later TG 1), 1Z + HH, on the Eastern Front in the winter of 1943/1944.

During the second winter on the Eastern Front there was considerably more winter clothing and hot air generators available to the bomber units for their operations. Depicted here is an He 111 H-3

This operational aircraft belonging to Seeaufklärungsgruppe (Naval Reconnaissance Group) 130 (F7 +) nosed over on landing.

This photo was taken in the summer of 1943 at Orange, in the south of France, and shows an He 111 H-3 tow aircraft of the Starrschleppstaffel (Rigid-tow Squadron) based there.

Above: An He 111 H-20 prototype aircraft at Heinkel's Oranienburg factory, 1943.

Center: This He 111 H-3 (WerkNr. 6942) stemmed from the ATG production line and was assigned to air transportation after being mustered out by a bomber unit.

Below: He 111 H-20s over northern Italy, autumn 1944.

Left: The He 111 H-21 was only produced in small numbers. Some of the aircraft flew with KG 4 and KG 53.

Center: This He 111 H-16 being inspected by an American officer in 1945 belonged to KG 4..

Right: An He 111 H-20 being operated by a Transportgruppe in the East, winter 1944/1945.

This He 111 H-20 was captured in central Germany in early 1945.

Translated from the German by Don Cox

Front cover artwork by Steve Ferguson

Printed in China.
ISBN: 0-7643-0165-9
Library of Congress: 96-68380

This book was originally published under the title,
Flugzeug Profile-Heinkel He 111H Varianten
by Flugzeug Publikations.

We are interested in hearing from authors with book ideas on related topics.

Published by Schiffer Publishing Ltd.
77 Lower Valley Road
Atglen, PA 19310
Please write for a free catalog.
This book may be purchased from the publisher.
Please include $2.95 postage.
Try your bookstore first.

During the development of the He 111 H it wasn't just the defensive armament which was constantly being strengthened,; passive armor (around the dorsal gun position) was also improved.

An He 111 H-16 of Gruppe Uhl at Eggebeck in May of 1945. Notice the reinforced armor of the dorsal gunner's station.

Above: An He 111 of KG 27 prior to a mission.

Picture page 3: An He 111 H-11 during a transfer flight over the south of Germany.

Close-up of main spar attachment for "Klette Gerät"

He 111 H-8 with Klette Gerät

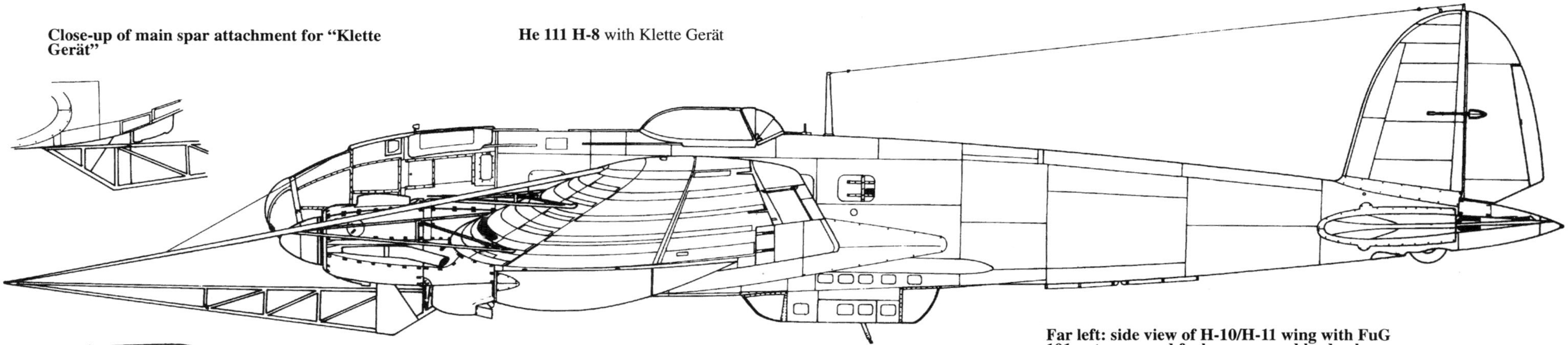

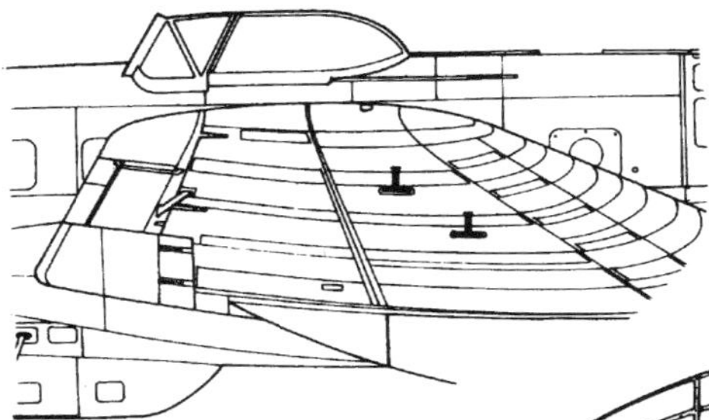

Far left: side view of H-10/H-11 wing with FuG 101 antennas and fuel emergency bleed valve

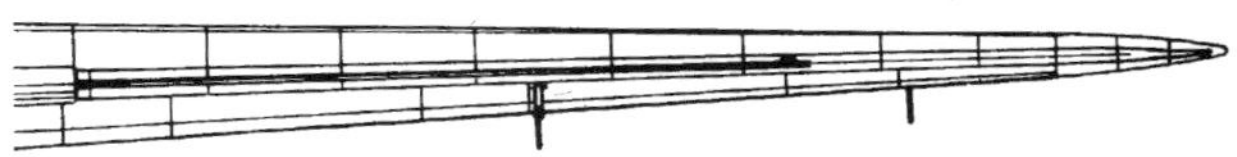

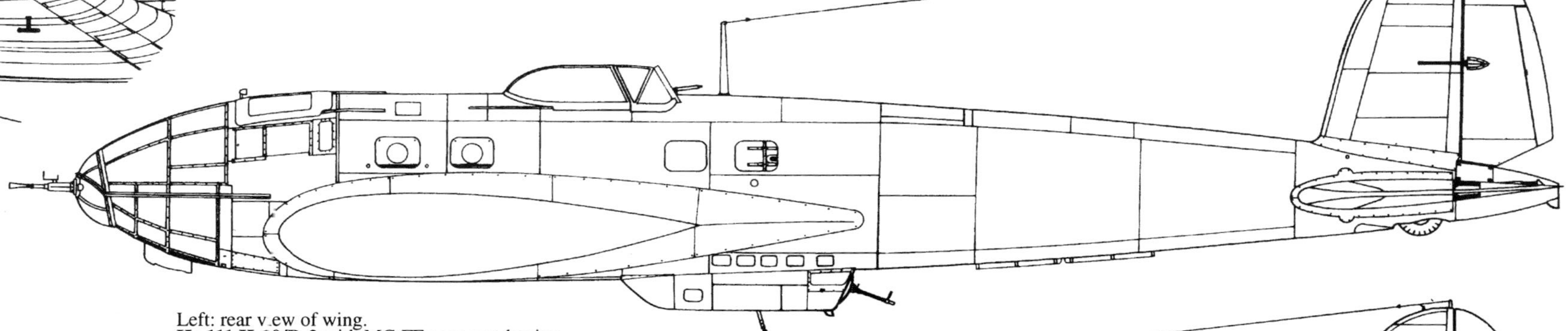

Left: rear view of wing.
He 111 H-10/R-2 with MG FF nose gun having flash suppressor for night operations.

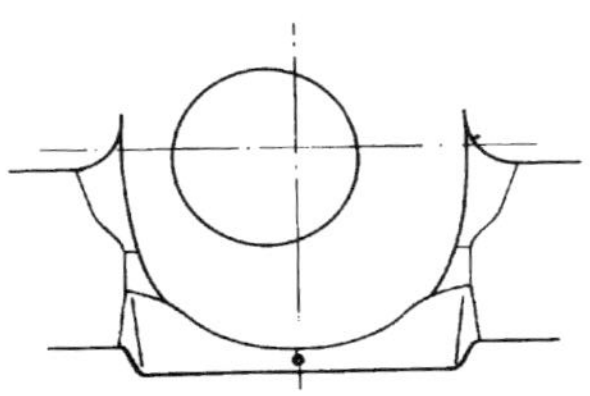

Front view of **H-11** showing special PVC ETC bomb rack.

He 111 H-11/R2

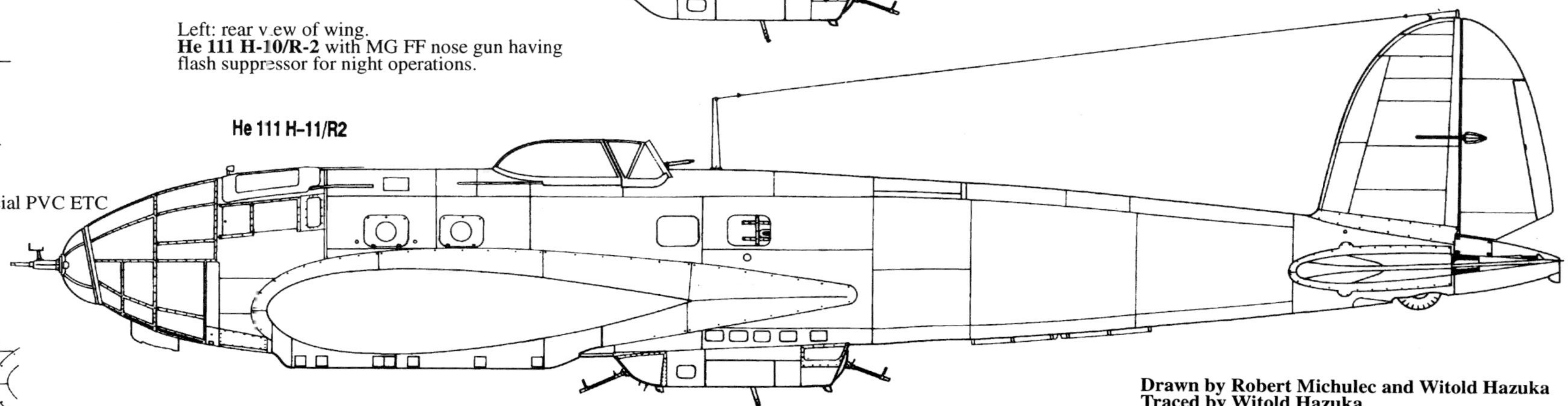

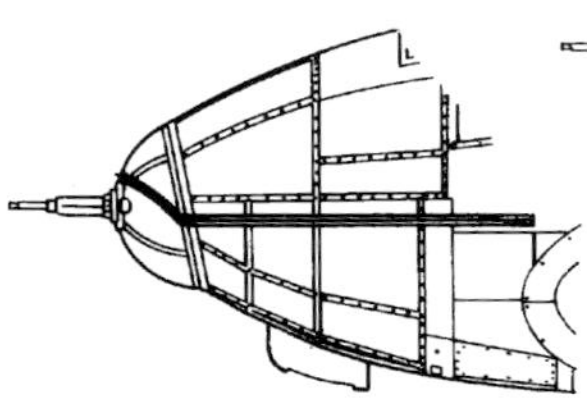

Scrap view of **H-11's** nose showing "Kutonase" for night operations.

Drawn by Robert Michulec and Witold Hazuka
Traced by Witold Hazuka

1/72 scale

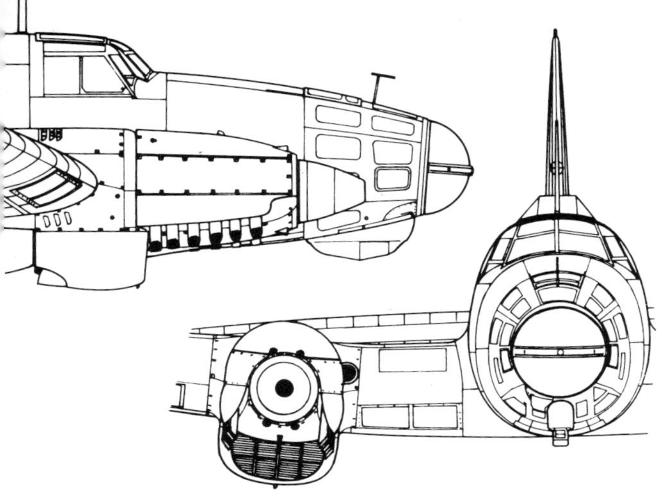

He 111 B-0 with DB 600A engines and surface oil coolers in wings

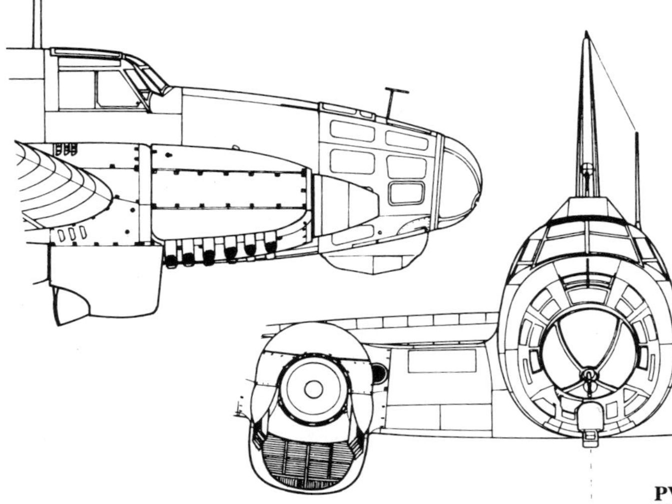

Late **He 111 B-1** with DB 600 CG engines and "Ikaria" nose turret; oil coolers moved beneath engine under glycol coolers

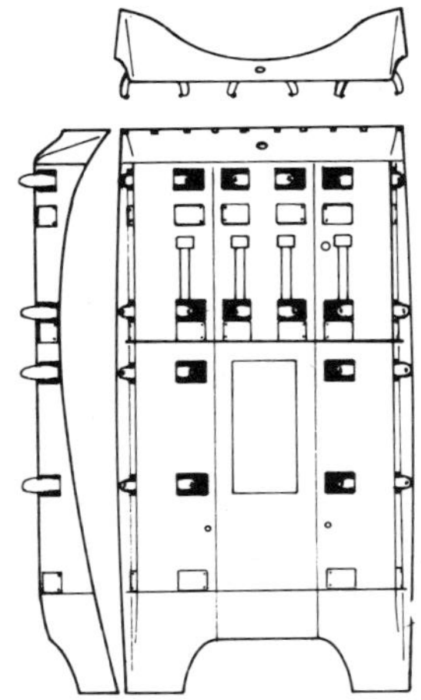

PVC ETC bomb rack for five 250 kg bombs

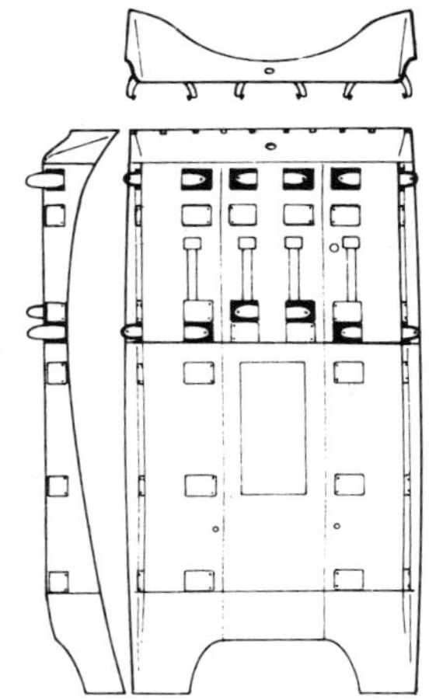

PVC ETC bomb rack for two 1000 kg and one 250 kg bombs

Exhaust variants 1/48 scale

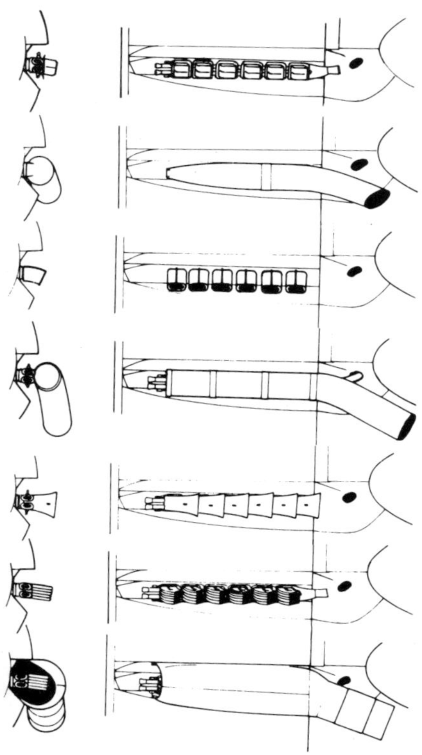

Late type (H-23)

Most common type (E/F-4/early H-series)

Very early type (E-series)

Flame damper found on H-series

Common type for P-series

Common type for H-series (mid-operational time period)

Flame damper for late H-series

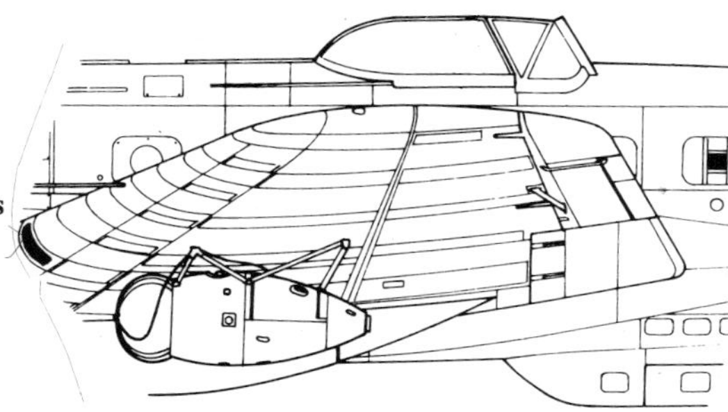

H-16 wing showing "R-Gerät" (Walter Rb 202 rocket-assisted takeoff engine)

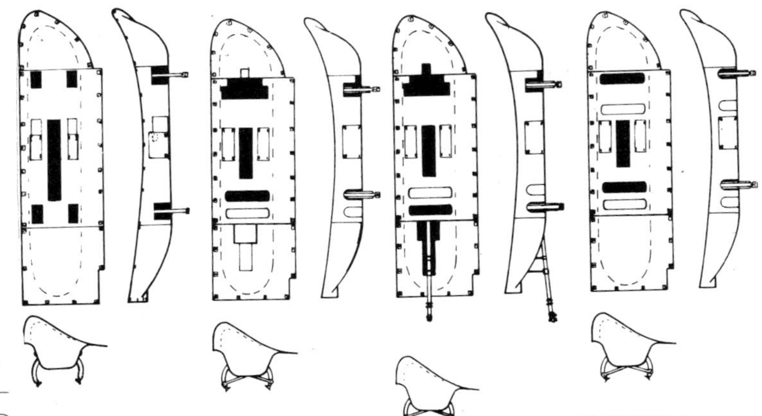

ETC 2000 underfuselage pylon

PVC 1006 B underfuselage bomb pylon

PVC 1006 B underfuselage torpedo pylon

PVC 1006 L underfuselage pylon

He 111 H-8 with alternative "Klette Gerät" installation

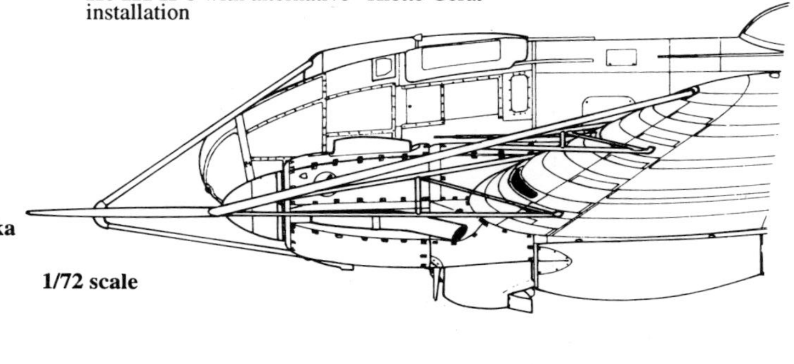

1/72 scale

Drawn by Robert Michulec and Witold Hazuka
Traced by Witold Hazuka

COWLING OF DAIMLER BENZ 601A ENGINE

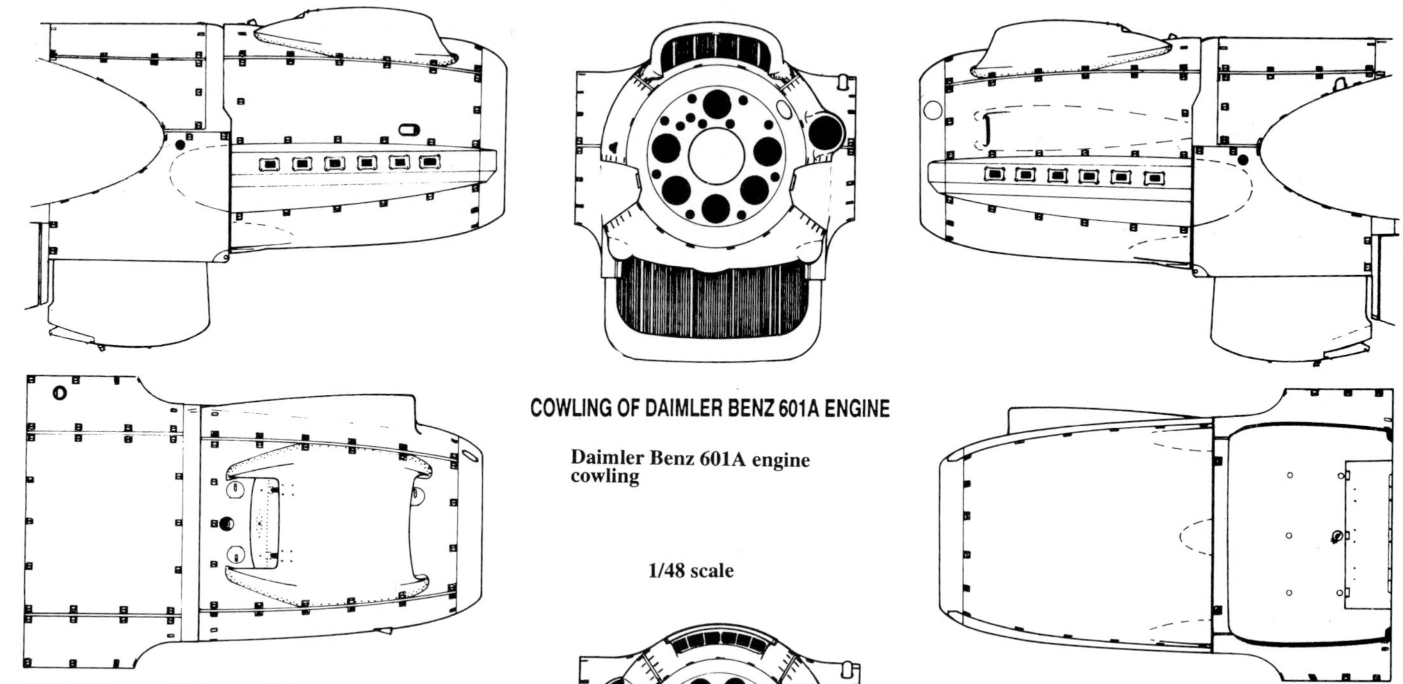

Daimler Benz 601A engine cowling

1/48 scale

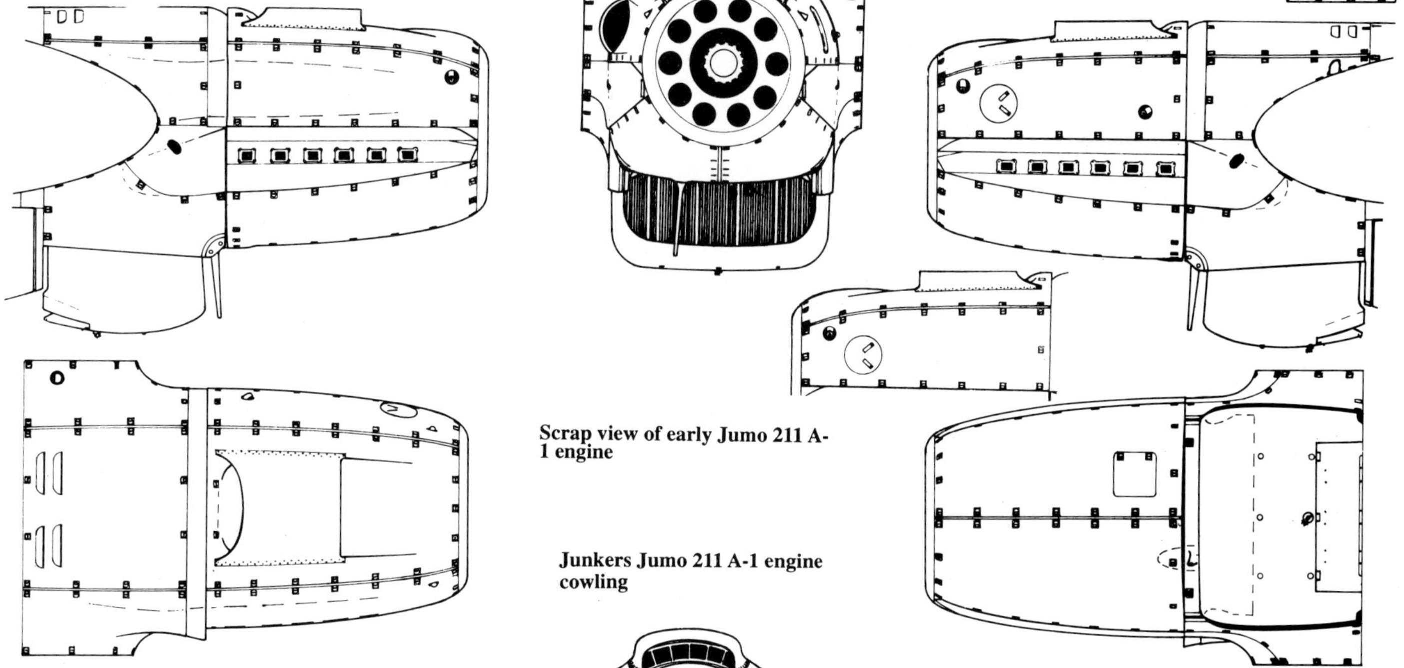

Scrap view of early Jumo 211 A-1 engine

Junkers Jumo 211 A-1 engine cowling

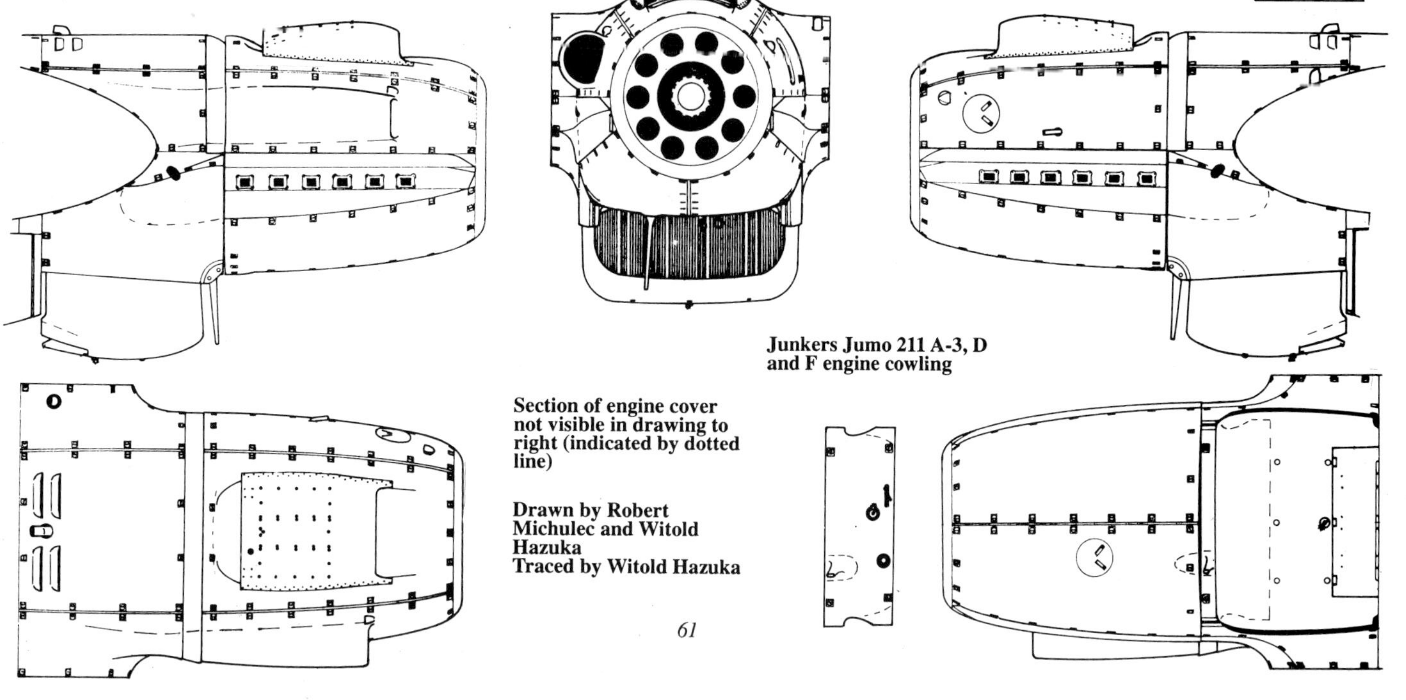

Junkers Jumo 211 A-3, D and F engine cowling

Section of engine cover not visible in drawing to right (indicated by dotted line)

Drawn by Robert Michulec and Witold Hazuka
Traced by Witold Hazuka

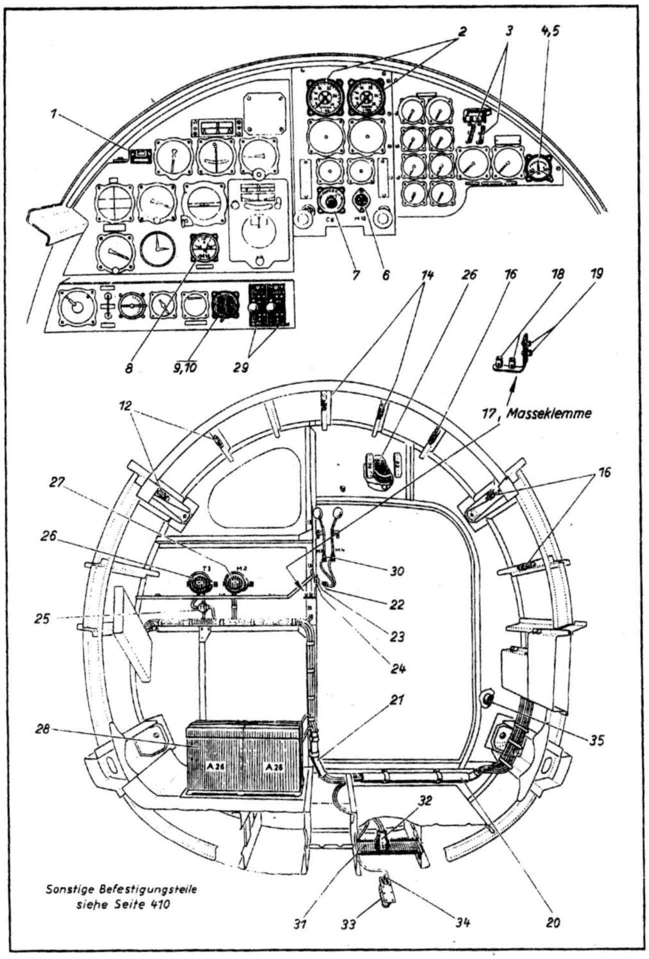

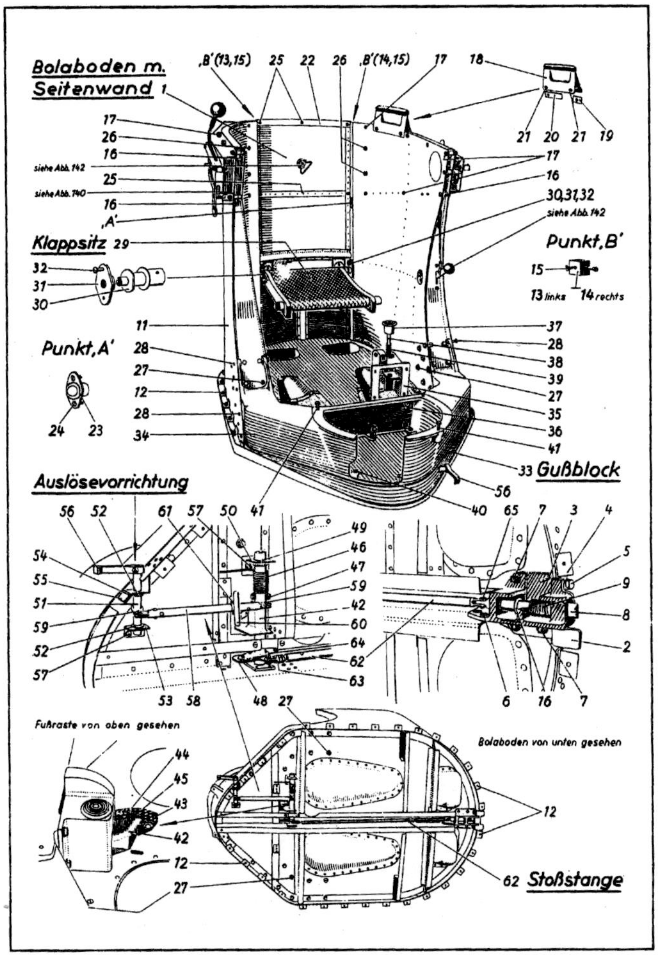

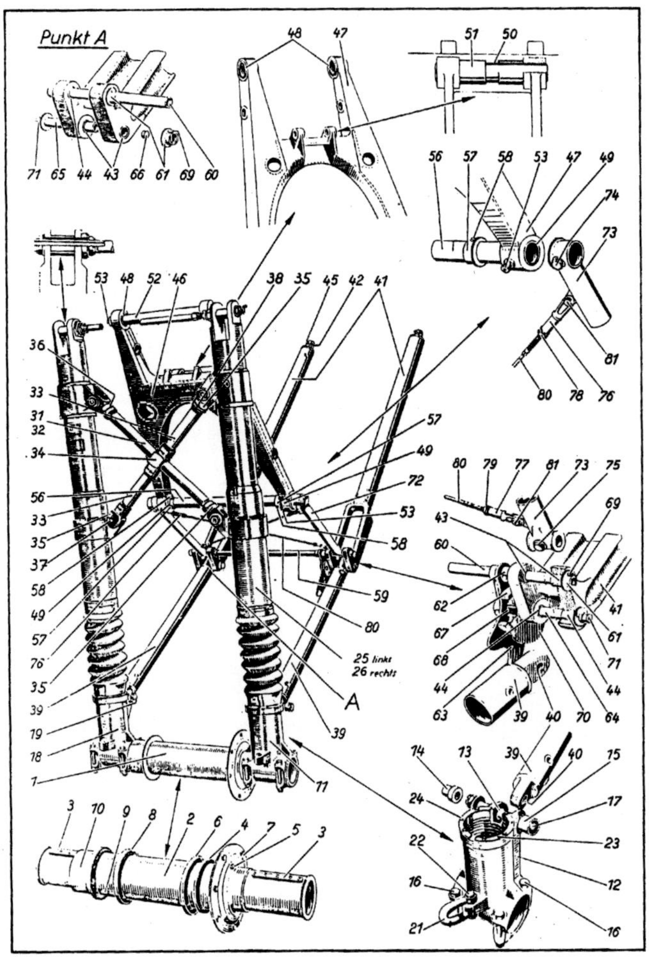

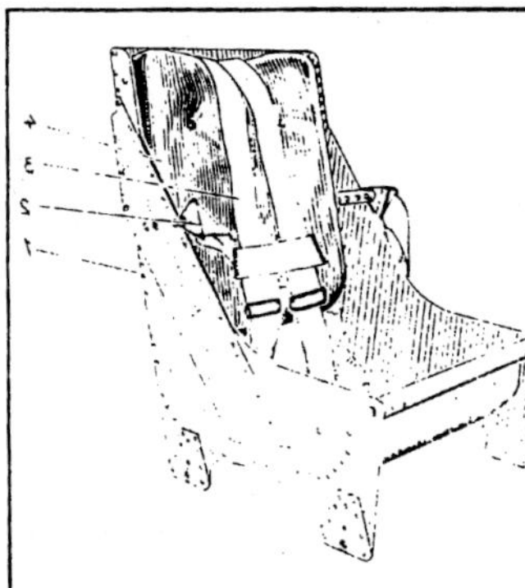
He 111 B, D, E, F, J pilot's seat

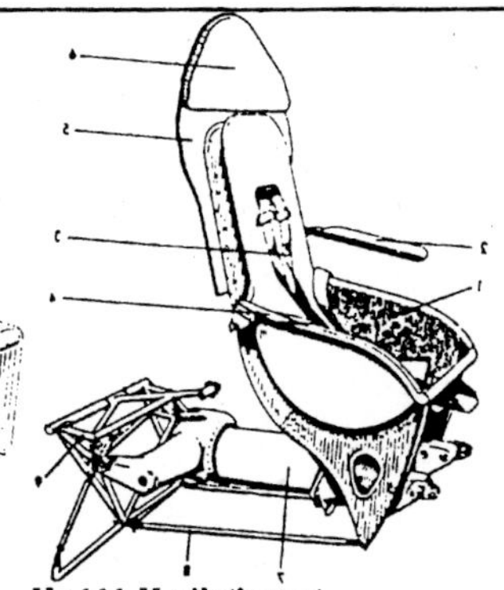
He 111 H pilot's seat

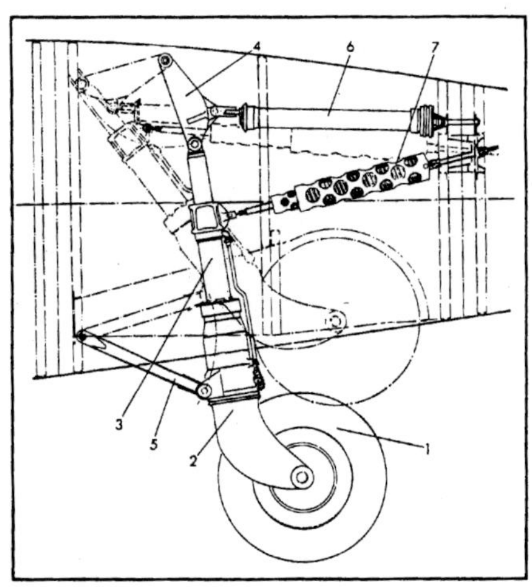

A-Stand

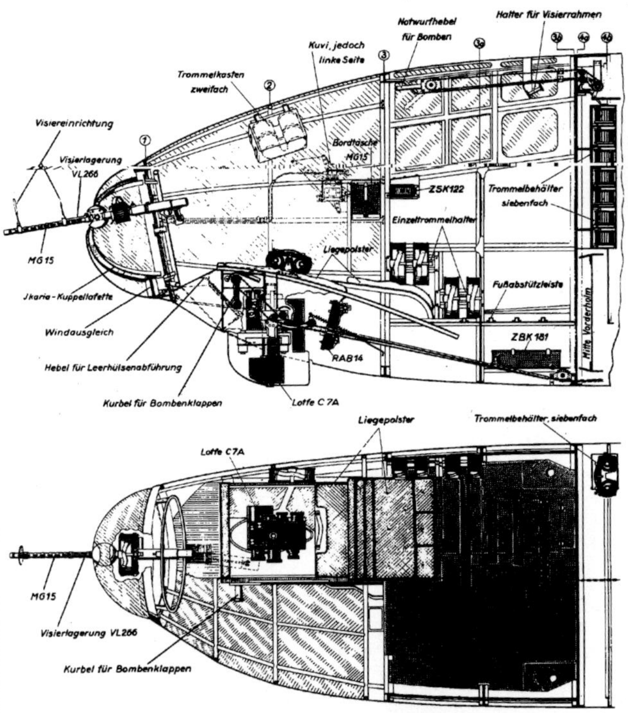

Waffenausrüstung in der Kanzel

Bombenausrüstung

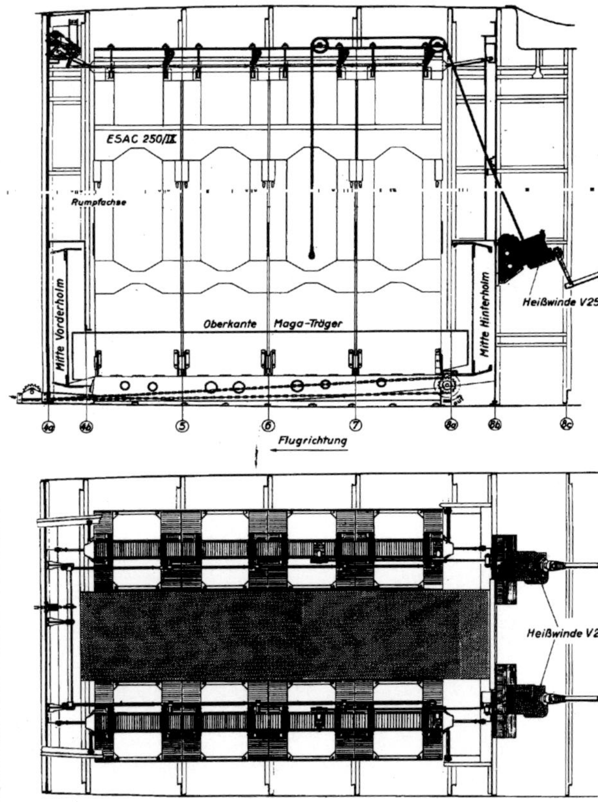

B-Stand

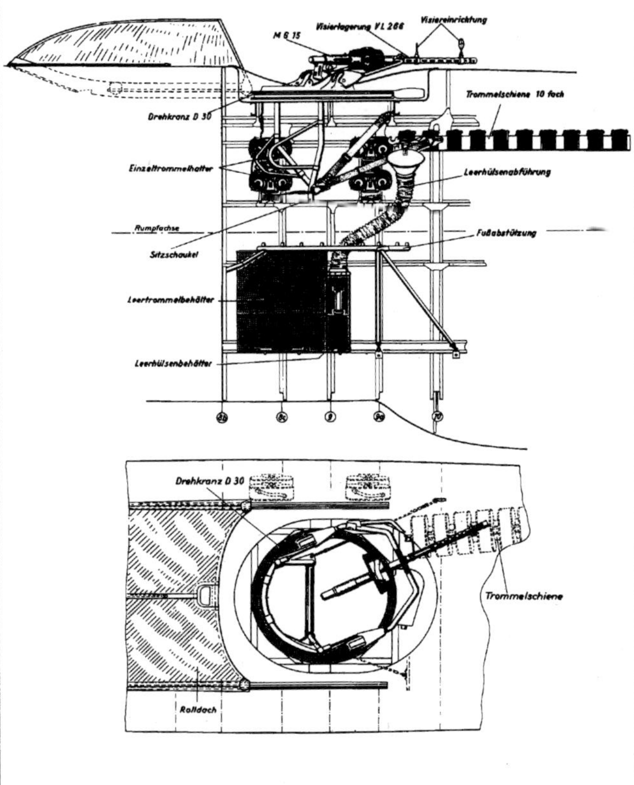

C Stand

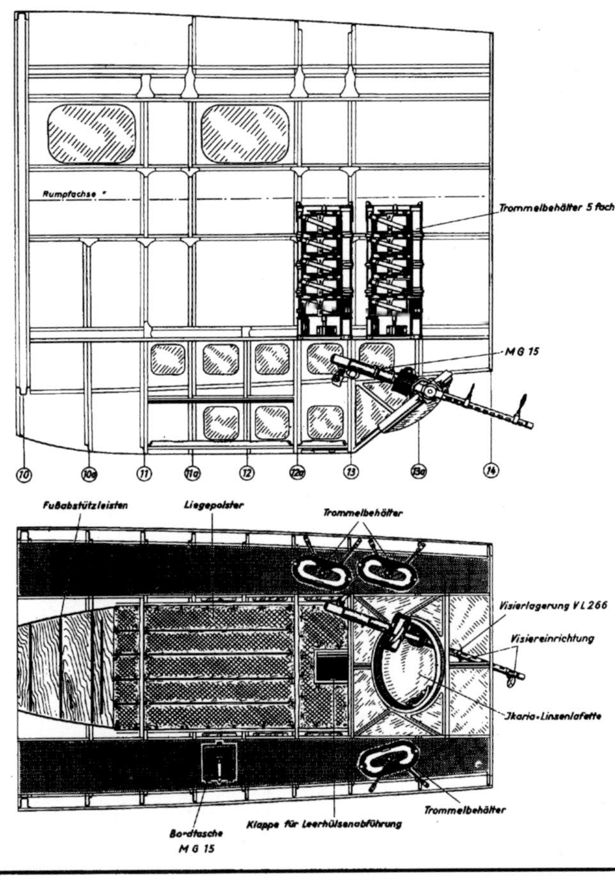

Heinkel He 111 H-6 during torpedo evaluation trials, with dummy torpedoes.